D0077837

Contents

The
Reference Shelf®

Guns in America

The Reference Shelf
Volume 89 • Number 1
H.W. Wilson
A Division of EBSCO Information Services, Inc.

Published by
GREY HOUSE PUBLISHING
Amenia, New York
2017

The Reference Shelf

The books in this series contain reprints of articles, excerpts from books, addresses on current issues, and studies of social trends in the United States and other countries. There
are six separately bound numbers in each volume, all of which are usually published in the
same calendar year. Numbers one through five are each devoted to a single subject, providing background information and discussion from various points of view and concluding with
an index and comprehensive bibliography that lists books, pamphlets, and articles on the
subject. The final number of each volume is a collection of recent speeches. Books in the
series may be purchased individually or on subscription.

Publisher's Cataloging-In-Publication Data
(Prepared by The Donohue Group, Inc.)

Names: H.W. Wilson Company.
Title: Guns in America / [compiled by] H. W. Wilson, a division of EBSCO Information
Services.
Other Titles: Reference shelf ; v. 89, no. 1.
Description: Amenia, New York : Grey House Publishing, 2017. | Includes bibliographical
references and index.
Identifiers: ISBN 978-1-68217-451-7 (v. 89, no. 1) | ISBN
   978-1-68217-450-0 (volume set)
Subjects: LCSH: Gun control--United States. | Firearms--Government policy--United
States. | Firearms ownership--United States. | Firearms--United States. | Violent crimes-
-United States.
Classification: LCC HV7436 .G86 2017 | DDC 363.330973--dc23

5

The Future of Guns in America

Preface

History of the Gun Debate—Right or Privilege?

Gunpowder was discovered in China in the ninth century CE, as a byproduct of experiments by alchemists searching for substances that could extend human life. Their discovery, ironically, would give rise to a lineage of weapons that made it far easier to bring about the opposite result. Gunpowder and cannons, which were also invented in China, were passed along the Silk Road trade routes, replacing siege weapons as the tools of mass warfare. Then, in 1364, a new arms race began with the invention of the first handheld cannon, which gave rise to the matchlocks (devices that connect a wick to a store of gunpowder), the wheel locks, the revolvers, the automatic pistols, assault rifles, and all other firearm families that followed suit. The invention of personal, portable firearms changed the world in myriad ways, fueling the foundation of new civilizations and the fall of others. The legacy of guns is complex and alternately heroic and horrific. The great cultures of Africa, Indonesia, and the New World fell because the indigenous inhabitants couldn't compete with the technological tools that accompanied European invaders and so guns powered colonialism, slavery, and genocide. As the oppressed co-opted the tools of the oppressors, guns also empowered rebellions and revolutions.

In many ways, guns and the United States evolved side by side. Historians believe that the first gun in the United States was likely an arquebus, or "hook gun," a long-barreled musket style weapon ignited by a matchlock. Spanish explorer Ponce de Leon's historic visit to the Florida peninsula in 1513 was most likely the first time anyone brought a firearm onto American soil, and the descendants of these early muskets would go on to play a major role in the foundation and expansion of the United States.[1] Guns were rare in the United States until the Civil War, but nevertheless played an important role in both the American revolution and the long genocidal struggle to wrest control of the land from its indigenous inhabitants.[2] From musket firing lines of the American Revolution to the iconic American gun makers—like the now famous Colt's Fire Arms Manufacturing Company or E. Remington and Sons—whose weapons became synonymous with the "Wild West" and American expansionism, guns were so essential to the foundation of the nation that the very idea of firearms, and public firearm ownership, has been conflated with American nationalism. This now venerable idea, that guns are emblematic of American identity, is the substrate of an equally old debate over the right of the state to limit access to dangerous technology in the interests of public welfare versus the right to own, carry, and collect weaponry for self-defense, hunting, entertainment, and to protect against governmental tyranny.

Rights and Privileges

In many nations, gun ownership is a privilege available only to those who can demonstrate behavior responsible enough to warrant being allowed to own a dangerous weapon. In the United States, gun ownership is a right, with the burden placed on the state to justify restricting weapon ownership, rather than on the individual to prove that he or she is qualified to own a weapon.

The right to own weapons is not unique to the United States. In the Roman Empire, free men (but notably not slaves) were given the right to own and carry swords for personal protection. Proponents of gun rights can find philosophical arguments to support their beliefs in the roots of Western culture, such as in the writings of British philosopher John Locke, who wrote that the "…right of self-defense is a fundamental law of nature."[3] The idea that the right to own weapons for self-defense is a God-given or natural law of humanity is one of the philosophical underpinnings of the gun-rights ideology. However, the argument that the proliferation of private weapons is an evil that governments and laws should seek to control is equally ancient. For instance, in number 15 in the 100 "principles of political wisdom," created in Ancient Greece states, "Let the laws rule alone. When weapons rule, they kill the law."[4] Western societies have a long, contentious history of weapons regulations and laws, with one of the earliest laws written in the English language being the English common law statute of 1328, which prohibited the carrying of dangerous or "unusual weapons" as a threat to the common peace.[5]

The idea of a "right to bear arms" was first codified in American law through the 1791 Second Amendment to the Bill of Rights. The Second Amendment was written less than a decade after the United States fought a war for independence with Britain in which citizen militias were an essential element in the American victory. At the time, Americans were fearful of foreign invasion and equally fearful of enabling the newly formed government to evolve into an organ of dictatorship, like the one colonists left Europe to escape. For some, especially in the American frontiers, they were also fearful of the hordes of "savage" tribes living in the rapidly expanding colonial territories and the allegedly dangerous wildlife that stalked American forests, deserts, and plains. From this phobic milieu, the founding aristocracy of the United States deemed it necessary to protect the right of the states to form and maintain militias and this right has been interpreted as the right for ordinary, US citizens, to purchase, keep, and carry firearms. In the defense of the Second Amendment, some display a tendency to treat the US Constitution with an almost fundamentalist fervor more typical of the approach towards spiritual scripture. Whether the rights of the constitution should be treated with this kind of absolutist approach is therefore a secondary subject within the gun-policy debate.

The oft-quoted and just as oft-debated phrase, "A well regulated militia, being necessary to the security of a free state, the right of the people to keep and bear arms, shall not be infringed…," has been interpreted to mean that the architects of the Constitution expressly forbade the United States government from passing any law that would interfere with an American citizen's right to own firearms. However, the federal statute refers only to "militias," and some argue that the document's authors only intended to allow states to build citizen militias, as a safeguard against federal tyranny and dictatorship. It is sometimes argued, therefore, that all citizens compose part of a "general militia," as opposed to a state's "select militia," and therefore that all citizens, as part of a public militia, are permitted to own and/or carry weapons under the Second Amendment. This interpretation is controversial, but has been favored by past iterations of the Supreme Court and so provides precedent for the legal gun debate in America.[6]

Gun Control Legislation in the States

In 1837, the state of Georgia, attempted to ban handguns out of concern over the rising number of gun homicides and injuries in the state, and this law became the first of many state laws challenged in the courts. In the 1846 case of *Nunn v. State of Georgia*, the Georgia Supreme Court ruled that the proposed ban violated Second Amendment freedoms and thus established a tradition of using the Second Amendment as justification to prohibit state efforts to enact gun-control legislation.[7] For nearly a century, the pendulum remained firmly with the gun-rights position until the rise of organized crime in the 1920s and the large number of civilian deaths in gunfights, helped to build a stronger and more committed lobby for gun control.

The National Firearms Act of 1934, which placed federal controls on the interstate sale and transport of firearms and prohibited certain types of firearms deemed too dangerous for citizen ownership, was the first federal law to limit Second Amendment freedoms. This was followed by the 1938 Federal Firearms Act, which required all firearms vendors to obtain a federal firearms license, to keep records of their sales, and made it illegal to sell weapons to those convicted of violent felonies. The first judicial test of these laws came in 1939, when Jack Miller, of Arkansas was arrested for transporting an illegal sawed-off shotgun across state lines. He argued that the arrest was a violation of his Second Amendment rights and won his case in the US District Courts. However, the US Supreme Court ruled in the 1939 case of *United States v. Miller* that there was no reason to believe a sawed-off shotgun was necessary for the preservation of a well-regulated militia.[8] The *United States v Miller* ruling established the idea that, while the Second Amendment gave citizens the right to keep weapons for hunting, self-defense, and to protect against tyranny, this freedom did not necessarily guarantee that all weapons should be equally protected.

Interest in gun control spiked again after the 1963 assassination of John F. Kennedy, and the revelation that assassin Lee Harvey Oswald killed Kennedy used a mail-order gun he obtained through an ad in the National Rifle Association's magazine, *American Rifleman*. The 1968 Gun Control Act was an effort to make it more difficult for individuals to obtain guns and included stronger laws regarding gun licensing. After the attempted assassination of Ronald Reagan, which resulted in the accidental shooting of former Press Secretary James Brady, there was another push for gun control, resulting in the 1993 Brady Handgun Violence Act, which established the National Instant Criminal Background Check System and required gun sellers to check the identity of all purchasers against the system before selling them a weapon. The law, signed by Bill Clinton with Reagan's support, was one of two major pieces of federal legislation passed during Clinton's two administrations. In 1994, Clinton's Violent Crime Control and Law Enforcement Act banned the manufacture, use, import, and possession of 19 different types of assault weapons.

Since the mid-90s, the pendulum has swung in the favor of gun rights. Clinton's assault weapons ban of 1994 expired in 2004, and President George W. Bush chose not to renew it. In 2008, the Supreme Court revisited the issue for the first time since 1939, striking down a Washington D.C. law banning handgun ownership. It was a major victory for gun-rights advocates and represented the first time that the Supreme Court sided with the personal liberties interpretation of the Second Amendment over the rights of states to control gun ownership.

Regulation of Dangerous Technology

One of the widely repeated slogans of America's National Rifle Association—Guns don't kill people, people kill people—is intended to highlight the fact that banning the tools used in murders will not address the reasons that people want to, and do, murder each other. It is also meant to argue that a gun is just like any other tool or weapon, having no inherent moral value except in how the tool is used or misused. The "guns are just tools" argument is factually verifiable and logically defensible, but it is equally true that guns, unlike many other types of tools that are legal for citizen ownership, are inherently and intentionally deadly by design.

When the number of accidental gun deaths each year is combined with homicides, justifiable killings, and suicides, the number of individuals killed with guns each year is roughly similar to the number who die in motor vehicle accidents.[9] This statistic does not provide justification for the prohibition of all firearms, any more than it provides justification for the prohibition of motor vehicles, but it does show that guns, like motor vehicles, are dangerous devices.

Because motor vehicles are dangerous, governments place restrictions on the use of motor vehicles, requiring individuals who own or operate them to demonstrate—not just once, but periodically throughout their lives—that they are aware of motor vehicle laws and are physically and mentally capable of safely operating a vehicle. Furthermore, individuals who demonstrate an inability to follow the laws or who are discovered operating motor vehicles in an unsafe manner, may be temporarily or permanently banned from using or owning a vehicle and may have their vehicles, despite being private property, confiscated for the benefit of the general public. Such measures far from guarantee against motor vehicle misuse, death, or injury, but are deemed a necessary violation of personal freedoms in the interest of enhancing public safety. While it might therefore be correct to state that guns are simply tools and that the only danger from guns is in how they are used, it is equally correct to state that guns are inherently dangerous tools and that there is a justifiable right for citizens to demand that the states and the federal government be allowed to place restrictions on firearm ownership and use in the interest of public safety.

Micah L. Issitt

Works Used

Acosta, Luis. "United States: Gun Ownership and the Supreme Court." *LOC*. Library of Congress. July 2008. Web. 25 Dec 2016.

Belleseiles, Michael A. *Arming America: The Origins of a National Gun Culture*. New York: Alfred A. Knopf, 2000.

Brabner-Smith, John. "Firearm Regulation." *Law and Contemporary Problems*. Vol. 1, No. 4, 1934, 400–14. Pdf. 25 Dec 2016.

DeBrabander, Firmin. *Do Guns Make Us Free?: Democracy and the Armed Society*. New Haven, CT: Yale University Press, 2015.

"Growing Public Support for Gun Rights." *Pew Research*. Pew Research Center. Dec 10 2014. Web. 25 Dec 2016.

Halbrook, Stephen P. *The Founders' Second Amendment: Origins of the Right to Bear Arms*. Chicago: Ivan R. Dee, 2008.

Ingraham, Christopher. "Guns Are Now Killing as Many People as Cars in the U.S." *Washington Post*. Nash Holdings. Dec 17 2015. Web. 28 Dec 2016.

Lane, Melissa. "How the Greeks Viewed Weapons." *The New Yorker*. Condé Nast. Feb 1 2013. Web. 25 Dec 2016.

Ruben, Eric M. and Saul Cornell. "Firearm Regionalism and Public Carry: Placing Southern Antebellum Case Law in Context." *The Yale Law Journal*. Vol. 125. Sep 25, 2015. Web. 25 Dec 2016.

Weeks, Linton. "The First Gun in America." *NPR*. National Public Radio. Apr 6 2013. Web. 25 Dec 2016.

Notes

1. Weeks, "The First Gun in America."
2. Belleseiles, *Arming America*.
3. DeBrabander, *Do Guns Make Us Free?*
4. Lane, "How the Greeks Viewed Weapons."
5. Brabner-Smith, "Firearm Regulation."
6. Halbrook, *The Founders' Second Amendment*, 300–10.
7. Ruben and Cornell, "Firearm Regionalism and Public Carry.
8. Acosta, "United States: Gun Ownership and the Supreme Court."
9. Ingraham, "Guns Are Now Killing as Many People as Cars in the U.S."

1
The Ideology of Guns

Nicholas Kamm/AFP/Getty Images

US Democratic Representative from Georgia John Lewis speaks as members and supporters of the US Congressional LGBT Equality Caucus hold pictures of victims of the Pulse nightclub attack, one month after a gunman killed 49 people at the club in Orlando, Florida, during a vigil in Washington, DC, on July 12, 2016.

Firearms in America: Personal Liberty Versus Collective Responsibility

Living with other people has tremendous advantages. Societies enable humans to achieve more than they could alone and to live lives that would be impossible for those forced to concentrate their daily efforts on subsistence. However, there are also necessary costs to living in societies. Building a community requires that individuals make sacrifices and the distinctly human process of establishing laws, necessarily involve balancing personal liberty with collective responsibility. For instance, on the issue of environmental management, laws represent a middle ground between the right of individuals to own property and to consume, pollute, or destroy natural resources found on their property and environmentally linked to their activities within their property, with the rights of the community to protect some natural resources or portions of the collective territory against environmental destruction. The gun-policy debate essentially covers this same ideological divide and, at the polar opposites of the debate, are the proposal that owning guns is a personal freedom afforded by the Constitution, reflecting the natural right of self-defense against violence and/or tyranny and the proposal that the community has the right to restrict certain freedoms in the public interest.

The Dangers of Tyranny

The United States was founded by individuals seeking to escape the tyranny and religious persecution of the British aristocracy and grew to its current state by embracing political, religious, and ethnic exiles looking to escape economic and social stagnation and oppression in their native countries. Fear of government tyranny is central to the imagined American ethos and there are many in the gun-rights lobby who continue to tout the dangers of government oppression as one of the primary justifications for gun ownership. At the ideological extreme are members of America's more than 270 (as of 2015) militia organizations, like the Georgia Security Force, who train in the use of guns and collect arsenals of legal weapons for the purpose of defending against an imagined future war against a despotic American government. Some in these movements believe that the American government has already become deeply tyrannical and fear that big-government and Democratic candidates like Hillary Clinton are on the verge of abolishing the Second Amendment.[1] Such fears, which are factually unfounded and almost entirely the product of misinformation, surprisingly lead to vast increases in gun sales, as millions of Americans legitimately believe, despite a complete lack of evidence, that they are on the verge of losing the freedom to do so.

The militia movement tends to recruit through gun shows and gun-rights meetings and represents a small, extreme, and passionate part of the gun-rights movement. Gun-rights organizations like the National Rifle Association (NRA) do not disavow the militias and actively pander to conspiratorial and highly suspect justifications for gun ownership.[2] The threat of revolt against the government if and when the government tries to disarm citizens is not exclusively an extremist attitude. Former NRA president Charlton Heston popularized the slogan, "I'll give you my gun when you pry it from my cold, dead hands," which became a common phrase on NRA t-shirts, bumper stickers, and other merchandise into the twenty-first century.[3]

The idea that citizen arms are a deterrent against tyranny has become mainstream in the gun-rights lobby, and there are a series of widely shared quotes and memes claiming that despots like Hitler, Stalin, and Pol Pot used gun-control legislation to disarm the populace before transforming their societies into dictatorships. For instance, David Kopel, researcher for the pro-gun Independence Institute argued in a 2003 article that, "Simply put, if not for gun control, Hitler would not have been able to murder 21 million people." Is this statement true? No. Prior to taking over Germany, Hitler's Nazi movement campaigned against gun-control legislation under the Versailles Treaty, and supported laws that liberalized gun ownership. The 1938 law typically used to justify the propagandistic statement about tyranny and gun control actually liberalized gun ownership for most Germans, though it made it illegal for Jews, convicted felons, and other enemies of the state to own weapons. This law also came *after* Hitler had come to power and after his dictatorship was well underway.[4]

Contained within the claim that gun control is a tool of dictatorship is the implication that politicians supporting gun control have fascist, dictatorial, or tyrannical leanings or, at least, that they are unconsciously part of a governmental system that is insidiously leaving the nation more vulnerable to tyranny. While there are many legitimate arguments in favor of gun rights, the argument that gun control is inherently tyrannical or is a preamble for tyranny is fallacious and unfounded. All gun-control legislation in United States' history has been motivated by the desire to prevent crime and enhance public safety and there is no legitimate evidence to support the belief that gun control is being purposefully used to erode the power of the people to resist governmental oppression.

The War for Public Opinion

In 2013, for the first time since research organizations began recording public opinion on firearms ownership in 1978, more Americans favored gun rights (52%) than gun control (46%).[5] However, the American public overwhelmingly agrees that firearms are too easy to obtain and that not enough has been done to prevent dangerous individuals from obtaining guns. Across partisan lines in 2016, for instance, more than 83 percent of voters believed that background checks should be required for all gun sales, including those that take place at gun shows or through private transactions, which are sometimes exempt from federal background check requirements.[6]

Essentially then, a majority of Americans embrace private gun ownership, but a far larger majority believes that gun laws and regulations are insufficient to protect the public from the dangers of guns.

In the 1980s and '90s, a vast majority of Americans favored gun control and only a small minority advocated for more permissive gun rights. The subsequent shift away from gun control is therefore subject of significant interest to criminologists and social scientists. In 2015 and 2016, industry reports indicated that Americans were purchasing firearms at record rates and reports have also shown that gun purchases spike after media coverage of mass shootings, such as the Orlando nightclub shooting in 2016. Some have speculated that the rise of radical conservativism—with extremist organizations like Al-Shabaab, the Islamic State, and the US Militia Movement regularly appearing on television and in print media—has created the perception that any individual or community is potentially a target for an extremist attack and has therefore motivated increased interest in gun ownership for self-protection.

The gun-rights lobby, influenced heavily by the commercial gun industry, has passionately promoted the idea that legal gun ownership makes individuals, communities, and families safer from violent crime. An April 2016 poll from Rasmussen Reports found that 66 percent of Americans believed that self-defense was the primary reason for purchasing a firearm and, among gun owners, 63 percent felt safer having a gun in the household.[7] Concern over the threat of violent crime seems to have increased over the past two decades and yet, by any legitimate metric, crime rates have fallen by more than one-third over the same period, in what social scientists sometimes call the "Great American Crime Decline."[8] Despite arguments from the gun-rights lobby that legal gun ownership is the *reason* that crime rates have declined, there is no compelling evidence for this belief and numerous well-researched studies providing evidence that the reduction in crime is related to factors that have no connection to legal gun ownership. A lack of evidence does not necessarily mean that legal guns are not useful for self-defense, but simply means that gun rights proponents cannot, given current evidence, legitimately claim that legal gun ownership has reduced crime.[910]

Numerous polls have found that Americans, as a whole, vastly overestimate the frequency of violent crimes and one of the reasons why American's perception fails to match reality might be found in media-marketing strategies. News outlets, especially television and Internet news sources, provide disproportionate coverage of violent crime because such coverage draws higher ratings and stronger interest. This phenomenon creates a "saliency bias" in the American public where Americans worry most about the top stories on the news, despite the fact that the top stories might not represent the most pressing threats or concerns facing the average citizen, inadvertently creating false perceptions about the state of American society.[11]

Legitimacy of Information

As the debate over guns and self-defense shows, there are many facets of the gun debate for which current data is insufficient. In trying to learn about the issue, interested individuals are often faced with information promoted by ideological lobbyist groups that too often use misinformation, poor scholarship, and biased interpretations of statistics to support their viewpoint. The most ardent advocates of gun control sometimes publish misleading studies on the prevalence of gun violence that fail to differentiate between gun crime, suicide, and justified shootings, thus exaggerating the scope of the gun-violence problem in America. Similarly, gun-rights advocates regularly publish articles rife with misinformation that underestimate the frequency of gun violence and overstate the positive effects (potential or realized) of legal gun ownership. Those interested in reliable data on the issue need to approach popular news items and especially items posted on social media or Internet news sites as potentially suspect, and take time to evaluate the statistics, quotes, and information provided in support of one argument or the other. Internet searches and patient evaluation can often help a reader to differentiate between a legitimate work of journalism or scholarship and one with far less grounding in legitimate data. Citizens should likewise encourage government and private studies on key issues, helping to arm those involved in the debate with better, more comprehensive information. Like many of America's most contentious issues, gun policy requires a compromise between personal liberty and collective responsibility and, though there may always be those unwilling to compromise, most Americans are willing to see the topic through a more moderate lens, preserving the right to weapons ownership while making responsible decisions to protect the public from a potentially dangerous technology.

Micah L. Issitt

Works Used

Cassidy, John. "The Saliency Bias and 9/11: Is America Recovering?" *The New Yorker*. Condé Nast. Sep 11 2013. Web. 26 Dec 2016.

Childress, Sarah and Chris Amico. "How Loaded Is the Gun Lobby?" *PBS Frontline*. Public Broadcasting Service. Jan 6 2015. Web. 25 Dec 2016.

"Firearms and Violence: A Critical Review." *NAP*. National Academies Press. National Research Council. 2004. Pdf. 29 Dec 2016.

Foran, Clare. "The Missing Data on Gun Violence." *Atlantic*. Atlantic Monthly Group. Jan 21 2016. Web. 26 Dec 2016.

Ford, Matt. "What Caused the Great Crime Decline in the U.S.?" *Atlantic*. Atlantic Monthly Group. Apr 15 2016. Web. 26 Dec 2016.

Fortunato, David. "Can Easing Concealed Carry Deter Crime?" *Social Science Quarterly*. 2015. Pdf. 29 Dec 2016.

"Growing Public Support for Gun Rights." *Pew Research*. Pew Research Center US Politics and Policy. Dec 10 2014. Web. 25 Dec 2016.

Harcourt, Bernard E. "On Gun Registration, the NRA, Adolf Hitler, and Nazi Gun Laws: Exploding the Gun Culture Wars (A Call to Historians)." *Fordham Law Review*, Vol. 73, No. 2, Art. 11, 2004, 653–80.

"Opinions on Gun Policy and the 2016 Campaign." *Pew Research*. Pew Research Center US Politics & Policy. Aug 26, 2016. Web. 25 Dec 2016.

Raymond, Emilie. "From My Cold, Dead Hands: Charlton Heston and American Politics." Lexington, KY: University Press of Kentucky, 2006.

"Why Are Americans Buying So Many Guns?" *Rasmussen Reports*. Rasmussen Reports, LLC. Apr 13 2016. Web. 26 Dec 2016.

Wilson, Jason. "Extremist Militias Recruiting in Fear of Clinton Winning Election, Activists Say." *The Guardian*. Guardian News and Media. Oct 18 2016. Web. 28 Dec 2016.

Zucchino, David. "A Militia Gets Battle Ready for a 'Gun-Grabbing' Clinton Presidency." *New York Times*. New York Times Co. Nov 4 2016. Web. 25 Dec 2016.

Notes

1. Wilson, "Extremist Militias Recruiting in Fear of Clinton Winning Election, Activists Say."
2. Zucchino, "A Militia Gets Battle Ready for a 'Gun-Grabbing' Clinton Presidency."
3. Raymond, *From My Cold, Dead Hands*.
4. Harcourt, "On Gun Registration, the NRA, Adolf Hitler, and Nazi Gun Laws."
5. "Growing Public Support for Gun Rights," *Pew Research*.
6. "Opinions on Gun Policy and the 2016 Campaign," *Pew Research*.
7. "Why Are Americans Buying So Many Guns?," *Rasmussen Reports*.
8. Ford, "What Caused the Great Crime Decline in the U.S.?"
9. "Firearms and Violence: A Critical Review," *National Academy of Science*.
10. Furtunato, "Can Easing Concealed Carry Deter Crime?"
11. Cassidy, "The Saliency Bias and 9/11: Is America Recovering?"

Gun Debate: Is Price of an Armed America a More Dangerous America?

By Patrick Jonsson
Christian Science Monitor, February 2, 2014

The number of Americans asserting their right to carry concealed guns has exploded —from less than a million a few decades ago to as many as 11 million now. There's evidence that gun prevalence can deter crime, but preventable tragedies perturb.

Charles Ingram and Robert Webster were neighbors in Florida, but friends said the two older men had little love for each other and often quarreled. On a spring day in 2010, the two men, both gun enthusiasts who had state permits to carry concealed weapons, got into another argument across their lawns.

This time, police later said, both men pulled out their weapons. When Mr. Webster began approaching, Mr. Ingram raised his gun, as did Webster. Two shots rang out simultaneously, and both men fell. Webster died almost instantly, Ingram less than a month later.

That "Deadwood"-style neighborhood gunfight is one of 555 examples compiled by advocates of gun control detailing how the mere presence of legal guns can turn mundane moments into tragedies—sobering rebuttals against the estimated tens of thousands of times a year Americans brandish guns in self-defense to thwart crimes in progress.

In a country that witnesses bloody gun violence of all kinds on a daily basis, Ingram and Webster were part of a growing cohort, a sort of standing militia of what concealed-carry advocates say are between 8 million and 11 million citizens carrying concealed guns in public in the name of protecting themselves and those around them.

Less than two decades ago, fewer than a million Americans carried concealed weapons, and they were mostly ex-police, ex-military, or owners of cash businesses.

Now, as more states expand open and concealed-gun carry to include bars, churches, airports, and college campuses, such tragedies highlight the life-and-death stakes of living in a more heavily armed America.

Complicating this rise of the concealed gun in America, new research on the psychology of what is called "embodied cognition" suggests that simply the act of holding a gun shades one's perceptions, sometimes at odds with reality.

To opponents of concealed carry, such research suggests that a toxic mix of politics and paranoia, added to 30 ounces of chromed steel tucked legally under a belt at Wal-Mart, ultimately equals a scarier and more dangerous society.

The Legal Right to Shoot

As of January, all 50 states, with various exemptions, allow people without serious criminal records or mental illness to obtain a permit to carry a concealed gun. That expansion of concealed carry coincides with the adoption of a new breed of self-defense laws that give armed citizens more—but not total—legal cover for shooting at fellow Americans.

In a recent paper titled "Second Amendment Penumbras," University of Tennessee law professor Glenn Reynolds points to major US Supreme Court decisions, including *District of Columbia v. Heller*, which in 2008 struck down the city's ban on handguns, as defining new parameters of self-defense and gun carry.

Until recently, Professor Reynolds writes, "gun ownership was treated as a suspect (or perhaps 'deviant' is a better word) act—one to be engaged in, if at all, at the actor's peril. But with gun ownership now recognized as an important constitutional right belonging to all Americans, that deviant characterization cannot be correct."

Illinois, the last holdout against concealed carry, was forced last year by the courts to allow it. A majority of states now have "shall issue" laws in which the state must award a permit if an applicant satisfies written requirements; other states have "may issue" laws that give police the authority to deny license applications.

The debate about whether the surge in public-carry laws heralds the dawn of a neo–Wild West era or simply restores the proper balance to gun rights has been punctuated by a string of incidents involving authorized gun carriers who killed fellow citizens over minor squabbles and preventable misunderstandings.

Florida, a pioneer in the liberalization of gun laws and a state where 1 in 19 people on the street is licensed to carry, has had several notable incidents involving concealed-carry permits in just the past three years: the fatal shooting in January at a Tampa movie theater, in which a well-regarded retired police captain shot a younger man, a father, in an argument involving texting and a thrown bag of popcorn; the killing of Trayvon Martin, in which a neighborhood watch captain shot the unarmed teenager after profiling him as a "punk" and scuffling with him; and an incident in which a white man with a concealed gun shot and killed a young black man in an argument over loud music (the shooter said he saw a gun; none was found).

Arguments for Concealed Carry

"I don't argue that there are no problems with [concealed-carry permit holders], but when you look at the data it's pretty hard to find any other group in the population that's as law-abiding as" permitted gun carriers, says John Lott Jr., an economist and gun-rights advocate and author of *More Guns, Less Crime*.

"The type of person who's going to go through the process of getting a concealed-carry permit is not the kind of person you have to worry about," he says. "They're law-abiding citizens who have a lot to lose if they make a mistake."

Statistics support Mr. Lott's assertion. The number of incidents in which concealed-gun carriers kill innocent people is a fraction of 1 percent of all gun-related homicides. In North Carolina, one of only a handful of states that reveals the identities of permit holders, 200 of the 240,000 concealed carriers (.08 percent) committed felonies of all types, including eight shooting deaths, in the five-year period ending in 2011. This compares with about 2.5 percent of voting-age Americans who have a felony rap sheet, according to The Sentencing Project.

The view of gun carriers as law-abiding citizens seems to have traction and correlates with increasingly positive public attitudes toward concealed carry. In 1999, an NBC News/Wall Street Journal poll found that 73 percent of Americans disapproved of making it easier for people to legally carry concealed weapons. In a Reuters/Ipsos poll last spring, 75 percent favored concealed carry by eligible citizens.

Another possible influence on public attitudes is the notion that an armed society is largely a polite society. Statistics suggest violent crime in the United States has gone down as more citizens either carry guns openly or concealed.

Using data reported by police to the FBI, the National Crime Victimization Survey reports that Americans used guns in self-defense 338,700 times over five years ending in 2011.

Concealed carry may have a deterrent effect as well. A recent Quinnipiac University study suggests that states with stricter concealed-carry laws have higher murder rates than states that are less restrictive, though it allows there could be other explanations for this difference.

Amplifying that point, a 2004 report by the National Research Council of the National Academies warned "it is not possible to determine that there is a causal link between the passage of right-to-carry laws and crime rates."

Brian Anse Patrick, a University of Toledo professor of communications and longtime concealed-carry permit holder, offers his own anecdotal evidence that concealed carry deters crime. In an interview he said he has personally brandished (but never fired) his gun several times to stop a possible crime. One example involved him displaying his handgun to a strange man who ran up to his car in the middle of traffic and began reaching into the back seat. The man backed off when he saw the gun.

Arguments Against

The "popcorn shooting" at the Tampa movie theater especially agitated pro-gun-control groups, who saw proof that even a gun carrier with decades of threat assessment experience could allow a situation to spiral out of control.

"Just because you're a law-abiding citizen today doesn't mean you're going to be one tomorrow," says Kristen Rand, legislative director at the Violence Policy Center in Washington, which keeps count of those killed by legal gun carriers in "non-self-defense" situations.

"In a lot of these cases," she says, "a shooter's life is ruined, an innocent person is dead, and there's a little girl with no father and a woman with no husband, and all because one guy believed the gun-lobby hype that 'I'm going to get this gun because someday I might need it.'"

The Violence Policy Center also marshals its own statistics on gun ownership and deaths, saying the total numbers of gun deaths, including suicides, are lower in states such as Massachusetts and Hawaii where there are fewer guns per capita than states with higher death rates, such as Louisiana and Wyoming.

For some gun-control advocates, the trend toward concealed carry also raises troubling undercurrents of race and class. They cihate words often seen on pro-gun Internet forums—the "good guy" versus "the thug," a term that commentators from the blogosphere to the sidelines of the NFL (Seattle Seahawks cornerback Richard Sherman) are calling the "new N-word."

While many new concealed-carry products—clutch holster bags, slimming underwear with holsters—at January's huge SHOT (Shooting, Hunting and Outdoor Trade) gun show in Las Vegas were for women, statistics from Arizona and elsewhere suggest it is primarily white men over 30 who are arming up.

Gun-control advocates consequently see the gun-carry movement as populated at least in part by white men who feel politically unempowered and who may be inclined to indulge in displays of extra muscle and power over their fellow citizens.

"There is a certain psychology at work with some who carry openly or concealed," writes columnist Stephen Lemons, in the *Phoenix New Times* newspaper. "I have seen it in the nativist camp, where these grizzled old white extremists try to provoke their enemies with guns on their hips, itching to blast someone."

> Now, as more states expand open and concealed-gun carry to include bars, churches, airports, and college campuses, such tragedies highlight the life-and-death stakes of living in a more heavily armed America.

While that may be harsh, even some concealed-carry proponents see a strain of disturbing behavior among some carriers.

"Acting like a deadly threat is imminent, walking around stores jerking your head around ... 'on a swivel,' planning your tactical movement from the gas pump to the cash register IS paranoid behavior, unless you live in Fallujah," writes one permit holder on a concealed-carry Internet forum. "Acting like every situation involves a critical threat is goofy.... Don't confuse life with movies."

Perhaps contributing to such confusion, guns can change people's perceptions at even deeper levels, according to recent research at the University of Notre Dame psychology department. The researchers had to get special permission from campus police to use replicas of handguns in a study that found that people holding a gun are more likely than those holding a ball to perceive objects in other people's hands as guns.

"Carrying a firearm changes what you can do in the world ... and that could potentially change the way you perceive and interact with people in the world," says James Brockmole, a Notre Dame psychology professor whose research has established a link between gun handling and "embodied cognition," the theory that objects encountered by the body unconsciously influence behavior. "People pay attention to the world differently if they're armed."

Where We're Going

However persuasive the recent instances of gun violence have been for gun-control proponents, they haven't changed dramatic trend lines in attitudes and gun ownership in America, which George Washington University law professor Bob Cottrol says has always been at least symbolically an armed society.

More than 300 million guns are distributed among about 40 percent of US households.

Since 9/11, the expiration of the federal assault weapons ban in 2003, and the social breakdown in New Orleans after Katrina, Americans have put aside post-Prohibition distrust of public gun carry and embraced the idea of it.

Surprisingly to some, 91 percent of 15,000 police officers polled recently by the PoliceOne organization also said they support citizens' ability to carry concealed weapons.

And while gun carry has always been popular in rural America, the current wave of concealed-carry seekers is largely urban professionals, says the University of Toledo's Professor Patrick.

Since the late 1990s no major federal anti-gun legislation has passed. Even the Sandy Hook massacre in Newtown, Connecticut, in 2012, in which 20 schoolchildren and six adult staff were killed, could not help President Obama and Democrats in Congress push through what they called "common-sense gun-safety reforms."

That failure last spring again drew attention to the National Rifle Association's ability to lobby lawmakers on a scale and intensity that pro-gun-control forces, even with the deep pockets of former New York Mayor Michael Bloomberg, could not match.

The NRA has long supported expanded concealed-carry laws, as well as anonymity for carriers. The nation's first recipient of a "shall issue" concealed-carry permit went to Marion Hammer, the NRA's longtime Florida lobbyist, after Florida passed its pioneering law in 1987.

While some states—notably Colorado, New York, and Connecticut—have tightened gun laws since Sandy Hook, most gun-related legislation in the states has decreased the barriers to carrying firearms in public.

That development has created some strange legislative bedfellows. Georgia Carry, a pro-gun group, lobbied last year to remove a rule banning anyone with a prior marijuana misdemeanor conviction from ever getting a permit to carry a concealed weapon in Georgia.

Lots of otherwise law-abiding middle-aged men were being denied gun-carry rights because of a commonplace youthful indiscretion, says Jerry Henry, the group's director.

"I personally don't understand why everybody's so scared of [guns]," he says. "They don't do anything by themselves."

Print Citations

CMS: Jonsson, Patrick. "Gun Debate: Is Price of an Armed America a More Dangerous America?" In *The Reference Shelf: Guns in America*, edited by Betsy Maury, 9-14. Ipswich, MA: H.W. Wilson, 2017.

MLA: Jonsson, Patrick. "Gun Debate: Is Price of an Armed America a More Dangerous America?" *The Reference Shelf: Guns in America*. Ed. Betsy Maury. Ipswich: H.W. Wilson, 2017. 9-14. Print.

APA: Jonsson, P. (2016). Gun debate: Is Price of an Armed America a More Dangerous America? In Betsy Maury (Ed.), *The reference shelf: Guns in America* (pp. 9-14). Ipswich, MA: H.W. Wilson. (Original work published 2014)

Most Americans Believe We Should Have Gun Regulation

Here Is Why Those Who Don't Are Winning the Debate

By Ann Christiano and Annie Neimand
The Conversation, July 4, 2016

There is a segment of the American population who believes passionately that guns are critical for personal protection against both violent individuals and governmental intrusion. They believe nothing should prevent them from getting the guns they need to do that.

There is another, larger group of Americans who believes passionately that we have created an environment that makes it far too easy for those who intend to kill to have access to all the firepower they want.

How could groups who hold these disparate views ever agree?

What's more: If most Americans believe we should have some gun regulation, why are those who don't winning the debate?

People on each side agree the threat from violence is real, but support different responses to that threat—either regulate the sale of guns or make sure a gun is in the hand of every good guy.

Winning Hearts and Minds

According to the Pew Research Center, "50 percent say it is more important to control gun ownership, just slightly more than the 47 percent who say it is more important to protect the right of Americans to own guns." However, 92 percent of Americans agree that there should be background checks for gun buyers. These numbers reveal a country deeply conflicted about the role guns play in keeping us safe.

No one wants to see more lives lost, and both sides make a case for public safety. Yet the discussion in support of commonsense gun laws tends to be shrouded in numbers, infographics, case studies and stories of lives lost, while those opposed make their case with powerful messages about threats to personal safety and liberty—messages that tap into cultural significance they associate with guns, as well as how they see themselves and their world.

Jonathan Haidt, a moral psychologist, says in his book *The Righteous Mind* that people form beliefs not through careful consideration of evidence but with gut emotional reactions to experience. They seek facts that justify their beliefs.

This means that people's beliefs about gun control are founded not in their careful consideration of available data, but in how they see the world.

At the University of Florida, we're building a curriculum and an emerging discipline called public interest communications that will help movement builders do their work more effectively. We bring together scholars, change makers and funders at an annual gathering called "frank" where people share the best of what they know about how to drive positive social change that reflects what the science tells us is in the public's interest.

Effective, strategic communication in the public's interest must be based in research. We spend our time digging for the best science that can help people driving change do so better.

One of the major themes that we have found in literature across a range of disciplines is the importance of cultural worldviews in building support for an issue.

Moral and social psychologists have studied how worldviews—cultural values, norms and how an individual sees the world—affect people's perspectives on politically charged issues like gun control. What they are finding is that your worldviews —more than your race, your gender, if and how you pray, how much money you have, where you're from or how you vote—are the single most accurate predictor of how you feel about guns.

Different Worldviews

Researchers have discovered that people who are more liberal tend to support solutions framed with language of equality and protection from harm. People who are more conservative tend to support solutions when they are presented in the context of protection for themselves and their families, respect for authority and preserving what is sacred. This gulf isn't limited to gun control. It holds up across a range of issues from climate change to marriage equality to health care.In one study, Donald Braman and Dan Kahan wanted to see if cultural worldviews influenced beliefs about who should have access to guns. They built two scales to measure participants' worldviews:

The first assessed how much participants were inclined toward
  * a hierarchical worldview, defined by deference to and respect for authority, or
  * an egalitarian worldview, defined by distrust of social hierarchies and support for social equality.

The second scale assessed how inclined participants were toward
  * an individualist worldview, defined by reverence for individual self-reliance, or
  * a solidaric worldview, defined by valuing the good of a community over individual opportunity.

Once they understood participants' worldviews, the researchers examined the influence of those views, as well as factors like religion and geography, on their attitudes toward gun control. They asked questions like whether participants supported a law that would require people to get permits before they could buy guns.

Not surprisingly, those who were more egalitarian and solidaric were more likely to support gun control. Those who were more respectful of authority were twice as likely to oppose gun control. Those who were more individualistic were four times as likely to oppose gun control.

Here is the important part: the participants' views on authority or their individualism were three times more significant than their faith, fear of crime or where they were from. And cultural worldviews were four times more powerful than political affiliation.

While cultural worldviews are not the sole predictor of gun control beliefs, they may influence them more than anything else does. What's important here is that we cannot make assumptions that people who oppose gun control belong to a particular faith, religion, politics or region. Looking at cultural worldviews offers a more promising approach.

> **This means that people's beliefs about gun control are founded not in their careful consideration of available data, but in how they see the world.**

In another study from Braman and Kahan, they make the case that arguments based in empirical claims for public safety are destined to fail because they don't tap into the symbolic meaning people associate with guns.

They write:

> [G]uns (at least for some) resonate as symbols of "freedom" and "self-reliance," associations that make opposition to gun control cohere with an individualist orientation … While control opponents see guns as celebrating individual self-sufficiency, control supporters see them as denigrating solidarity: guns are often equated with a hyper masculine or 'macho' personal style that many individuals, male as well as female, resent.

> In other words, the gun debate is destined to stagnate as long as those waving their empirical evidence in the air continue to ignore the symbolic meaning guns have for so many Americans.

A Positive Example

Here's an example of how one cause got it right: When Brian Sheehan, director of Ireland's Gay Lesbian Equality Network, developed a strategy that led Ireland to be the first country to support marriage equality, he and his team didn't root their message in the values of the people who already supported the issue—values like equality, fairness and social justice. Instead, they built a campaign for a particular audience that would be fundamental to passing the marriage equality referendum:

middle-aged, straight men. They crafted a message centered in this particular group's values of equal citizenship and family. Last May, Irish voters passed marriage equality by nearly two to one, making marriage equality real in a country where —just a decade earlier—it was a crime.

Imagine what the world could be like if we approached change by understanding the mindset of those who we hope to affect and engage them by talking about what matters to them. Could such an approach allow us to move forward as a society on the issues that will define us—even one as controversial and emotional as gun control?

Print Citations

CMS: Christiano, Ann, and Annie Neimand. "Most Americans Believe We Should Have Gun Regulation: Here Is Why Those Who Don't Are Winning the Debate." In *The Reference Shelf: Guns in America*, edited by Betsy Maury, 15-18. Ipswich, MA: H.W. Wilson, 2017.

MLA: Christiano, Ann, and Annie Neimand. "Most Americans Believe We Should Have Gun Regulation: Here Is Why Those Who Don't Are Winning the Debate." *The Reference Shelf: Guns in America*. Ed. Betsy Maury. Ipswich: H.W. Wilson, 2017. 15-18. Print.

APA: Christiano, A., & A. Neimand. Most Americans believe we should have gun regulation: Here is why those who don't are winning the debate." In Betsy Maury (Ed.), *The reference shelf: Guns in America* (pp. 15-18). Ipswich, MA: H.W. Wilson. (Original work published 2016)

Gun Research Faces Roadblocks and a Dearth of Data

By Meghan Rosen
Science News, May 3, 2016

Setting evidence-based policy isn't easy when research is underfunded and data are locked up.

Buying a handgun in Connecticut means waiting—lots of waiting. First comes an eight-hour safety course. Then picking up an application at a local police department. Review of the application (which includes a background check and fingerprinting) can take up to eight weeks. If approved, the state issues a temporary permit, which the buyer trades in at state police headquarters for a permanent one. Then it's back to the store for the gun.

Head west to Missouri, though, and buying a handgun is practically a cakewalk. Customers at Osage County Guns in Belle, Mo., for example, can walk into the store and walk out with a gun if they pass the FBI's instant background check, says John Dawson, the store's chief technical officer.

"If a person knew exactly what they wanted," he says, the store could, "in theory, complete the transaction in about 15 minutes."

Missouri and Connecticut have staked out opposite ends of the gun law spectrum. Connecticut didn't require handgun buyers to get a permit until 1995. Missouri had a tough law on the books, but repealed it in 2007. The states' laws have flip-flopped, making for a fascinating natural experiment on gun laws' effects on gun violence.

The states "had mirror image policy changes, and mirror image results," says Daniel Webster, a health policy researcher at Johns Hopkins University.

Flipping the laws was associated with 15 percent fewer gun suicides in Connecticut and 16 percent more in Missouri, a statistical analysis by Webster and colleagues, published last year in *Preventive Medicine,* estimated. Similar analyses by Webster in 2014 and 2015 indicated a 40 percent reduction in Connecticut gun homicide numbers, and an 18 percent rise in Missouri.

The evidence is very suggestive, says Harvard University researcher David Hemenway. But it's not extensive enough to persuade everyone—or to move national policy.

This article appears in the May 14, 2016, issue of *Science News* with the headline, "Misfires in the Gun Control Debate."

In fact, questions loom about the impact of all sorts of policies, from background checks to assault weapons bans to gun buybacks. That's partly because gun research faces roadblocks at every turn: Scientists have to deal with data shutouts, slashed funding and, occasionally, harassment.

For a few questions, however, researchers have come up with solid answers: There's a convincing link between gun availability and gun suicide, for one. And studies from the United States and abroad suggest that some gun laws do rein in gun violence. To make firm conclusions, though, scientists are desperate for more data.

But the US Centers for Disease Control and Prevention can't collect gun data like it used to, and information about guns used in individual crimes is locked up tight. Under current federal laws, Hemenway says, "It's almost impossible for researchers to get even the data that are available."

Locked Up

In a squat brick building tucked in the hills of Martinsburg, West Virginia, gun data are overflowing.

Thousands of cardboard boxes, stacked high in tidy columns, line the hallways of the federal government's National Tracing Center. In the parking lot, steel shipping containers hold even more boxes. Each box contains about 2,000 pages of gun purchase records. To trace a gun, the center's employees often search through these records by hand.

That's their job: tracking when and where guns used in crimes were originally purchased, and by whom. It's a huge undertaking: In 2015, the center, part of the Bureau of Alcohol, Tobacco, Firearms and Explosives, or ATF, received more than 373,000 gun trace requests from law enforcement.

Such a mass of data is a researcher's dream. But current laws keep gun traces secret. The agency shares traces only with law enforcement. The public can see just summaries or aggregate data.

Webster has used this data to paint a rough picture of how Missouri's repeal affected the flow of guns to criminals. In 2006, when buying a handgun required a permit, 56.4 percent of guns recovered by police had been originally sold by a Missouri gun dealer. In 2012, five years after the state nixed the permit requirement, the number rose to 71.8 percent, Webster and colleagues reported in the Journal of Urban Health in 2014.

The findings suggest that it's easier now for criminals in Missouri to get their hands on legally purchased guns. But Webster can't say for certain whether more guns are moving to criminals—or whether legal gun owners are committing more crimes. For that, he'd need to see the individual gun traces.

About a decade ago, researchers who wanted such detailed data could get it. "We'd just hand them a DVD," says ATF information specialist Neil Troppman. "Those days are long over."

A handful of laws snarl the process, from how a gun trace begins to who can see the data.

One big hitch in the system: Police officers who find a gun at a crime scene can't always look up the owner's name on a computer. That's because there is no national registry—no searchable database of guns and their owners. To set one up would be illegal. So police have to submit a request to the tracing center, which tracks the gun's movement from manufacturer or importer to dealer. Then the ATF can ask the dealer who bought the gun. If the dealer has gone out of business, ATF employees dig for the answer themselves, in old gun purchase records stockpiled at the tracing center. The process takes an average of five days. And after law enforcement gets the data, federal law makes sure no one else can see it.

Federal Constraints

In 2003, Congress unleashed a beast of a bill with an amendment that effectively tore out the ATF's tongue. The Tiahrt amendment was the first in a series of provisions that drastically limited the agency's ability to share its crime gun data—no giving it to researchers, no making it public, no handing it over under Freedom of Information Act requests (the public's channel for tapping into information from the federal government).

Funding for gun control research had dried up a few years earlier. There's no outright ban, but a 1996 amendment had nearly the same effect. It's known as the Dickey amendment, and it barred the CDC from using funds to "advocate or promote gun control." According to a 2013 commentary in *JAMA*, that meant almost any research on guns.

If the 1996 law's language was vague, Congress made the message clear by cutting the CDC's budget by $2.6 million—exactly the same amount the agency had spent the previous year on gun violence research. The funds were later reinstated, but earmarked for other things. So the CDC largely backed off, except for some basic tallying, says spokesperson Courtney Lenard, because of the funding cuts and because Congress "threatened to impose further cuts if that research continued."

In 2011, Congress hit the National Institutes of Health with similar restrictions. About a year later, President Obama tried to ease the choke hold: He ordered the CDC to research the causes and prevention of gun violence, and called on Congress to provide $10 million in funding. Finally, 17 years after the CDC cuts, news reports proclaimed that the ban had been lifted and research could resume. But Congress never authorized the money, and the CDC remained on the sidelines. This April, nearly 150 health and science organizations, universities and other groups signed a letter urging Congress to restore the CDC's funding.

Meanwhile, research on gun violence and gun control trudges forward: Researchers can sometimes convince law enforcement agencies to share data on guns linked to crimes, and grants can come from private foundations. Yet even with limits on research, the science in some cases is solid: A gun in the home, for example, increases the odds a person will commit suicide by about 3-to-1. Here, Hemenway says, "The weight of the evidence is overwhelming."

But how to use laws to reduce gun violence remains hotly contested, and opinions among the public, and even scientists, are polarized.

Critics of gun control laws think the matter is clear: Again and again studies show that gun control policies just don't work, says economist John Lott, who has written extensively on the subject. Take background checks, he says, "Given that these laws are costly, you'd like to believe there's some evidence that they produce a benefit."

Webster acknowledges the divisive split in opinions. "The vast majority of people are on one side of the fence or the other," he says. "They'll point to a study that is convenient to their political arguments and call it a day."

Bad For Your Health

For researchers who manage to navigate the legal tangles and funding troubles of gun research, actually doing the research itself isn't easy.

Unlike clinical trials in medicine, where scientists can give, for example, a cholesterol drug to half a study's participants and then compare the effects between users and nonusers, scientists studying gun violence can't dole out new handguns to one group and none to another and see what happens.

> 3.8x higher rate of suicides by gun in states with high versus low levels of gun ownership.

Instead, researchers turn to observational studies. That means looking at how—and if—suicides track with gun ownership in different groups of people and over time, for example. Finding a link between two observations doesn't necessarily mean they're connected. (People have linked the yearly number of Nicolas Cage movies to swimming pool drownings, after all.) But finding a lot of links can be telling.

For suicides, the link to gun access holds strong—among old people, young people, women, adolescents, "you name it," Hemenway says. Lots of guns means lots of suicides by gun, he says.

In 2007, Hemenway and colleagues examined gun ownership rates and statewide suicide data from 2000 to 2002. People in states with a high percentage of gun owners (including Wyoming, South Dakota and Alaska) were almost four times as likely to kill themselves with guns as people living in states with relatively few gun owners (such as Hawaii, Massachusetts and Rhode Island), the researchers reported in the *Journal of Trauma Injury, Infection and Critical Care*.

More recently, a 2013 study in Switzerland compared suicide rates before and after an army reform that cut the number of Swiss soldiers by half. After the reform, fewer people had access to army-issued guns—and the suicide rate dipped down by about two per 100,000 men age 18–43. That's about 30 men each year who didn't die from suicide, the study's authors estimated in the *American Journal of Psychiatry*.

A 2014 review of 16 such studies, published in the *Annals of Internal Medicine*, came to the same conclusion, again: Access to guns meant higher risk of suicide.

"The evidence is unassailable," says Stanford University criminologist John Donohue. "It's as strong as you can get."

Mental illness factors into suicide too, says Jeffrey Swanson, a medical sociologist at Duke University. (Some 21 to 44 percent of suicides reported to the CDC are committed by people with mental health problems.) And federal laws aren't particularly good at keeping guns away from mentally ill people. A 1968 law prohibits gun sales to a narrow slice of people with a history of mental illness, but it's easy for others to slip through the cracks. Even people the law does target can end up with guns—because states don't have to report mental health records to the FBI's national background-check system.

> **People with mental illness committed fewer than 5 percent of US gun killings between 2001 and 2010.**

"You've got tons of records that would disqualify people from buying guns," Swanson says, but they don't necessarily make it into the system.

Even if the United States had a perfect mental health care system and cured schizophrenia and bipolar disorder and depression, he says, the overall problem of gun violence would still exist. Mentally ill people just aren't that violent toward others, Swanson noted in the *Annals of Epidemiology* in 2015. In fact, people with mental illness committed fewer than 5 percent of US gun killings between 2001 and 2010, according to the CDC.

"People think that in order to fix gun violence, we need to fix the mental health care system," Swanson says. That's wrong, he argues. "It's a diversion from talking about guns."

Weak Laws

After Sandy Hook, San Bernardino and other high-profile mass shootings, people have been talking about what gun control laws, if any, actually work.

Unfortunately, there's just not enough evidence to make strong conclusions about most laws, Hemenway says. In 2005, for example, a federal task force reviewed 51 studies of gun laws, mostly in the United States, and came up empty-handed. The task force couldn't say whether any one of the laws made much of a difference. The efficacy of US gun laws is hard to pin down for two main reasons, Hemenway says: Gun laws aren't typically very strong, and studies tend to look at overall effects on violence.

One major study published in *JAMA* in 2000 analyzed suicide and homicide data from 1985 to 1997 to evaluate the impact of the Brady Act, a 1994 federal law that requires background checks for people buying guns.

Eighteen states and the District of Columbia already followed the law. So researchers compared suicide and homicide rates with those in the 32 states new to the law. If Brady curbed gun violence, those 32 states should see dips in deaths.

That didn't happen (with one exception: Gun suicides in those states dropped in people age 55 and older—by about 1 per 100,000 people).

"I don't think anybody was really shocked," Webster says. After all, Brady had a gaping hole: It didn't require background checks for guns bought from private sellers (including those at gun shows). The loophole neutered Brady: People who didn't want a background check could simply find a willing private seller. That's just too easy, Webster says: It's like letting people decide whether they want to go through the metal detector at the airport.

Like the Brady Act, the 1994 Federal Assault Weapons Ban didn't seem to do much to prevent violence, criminologist Christopher Koper and colleagues concluded in a 2004 report to the US Department of Justice. The law, which expired in 2004, imposed a 10-year ban on sales of military-style semiautomatic guns. These weapons fire one bullet per trigger squeeze and have features like threaded barrels (which can be used for screwing on silencers) or barrel mounts (for attaching bayonets). The 1994 law also banned most large-capacity magazines (storage devices that feed guns more than 10 rounds of ammo).

But like Brady, the ban came with a catch: It didn't apply to weapons and magazines made before September 13, 1994. That's a lot of exemptions. At the time, the United States had more than 1.5 million assault weapons and nearly 25 million guns with large-capacity magazines, reported Koper, of George Mason University in Fairfax, Va.

"The more complete the bans are, the better the effects seem to be," Donohue says. Take Australia: In 1996, the country enacted strict laws and a gun buyback program after a mass shooting killed 35 people in Tasmania. The ban made certain long-barreled guns illegal (including semiautomatic rifles and pump-action shotguns—weapons that let people fire lots of rounds quickly), and the country bought back and destroyed more than 650,000 guns.

With the law, Donohue says, "Australia effectively ended the problem of mass shootings."

And as economists Christine Neill and Andrew Leigh found, the law drastically cut down the number of gun suicides, too.

Tough Laws

Eleven years after Australia launched its tough gun control legislation, Neill, of Wilfrid Laurier University in Canada, and Leigh, then at Australian National University in Canberra, announced that the law might actually be saving lives.

Critics attacked. One petitioned Neill's university to reprimand her. Then they came for Leigh's e-mails. He had to hand over any that mentioned firearms or guns. Had there been anything improper—any whiff that the researchers were biased—Neill believes gun advocates would have pounced.

> To make firm conclusions, though, scientists are desperate for more data.

Neill and Leigh, now an Australian politician, had uncovered telling changes in different regions' suicide rates between 1990–1995 and 1998–2003. "Firearms suicides fell most in Tasmania, by a long shot," Neill says, almost 70 percent, the team later reported in 2010 in the *American Law and Economics Review*.

Australia's law, called the National Firearms Agreement, or NFA, applied to all of the country's states and territories, but some had more guns than others. Tasmania, for example, had the most guns bought back, Neill says: 7,302 guns per 100,000 people. More guns bought back meant bigger drops in suicide rates, she says.

Big Picture Only

Gun trace data are available to researchers only in aggregate. Researchers can look at the total number and the types of guns traced in a state. But they can't learn the where and when of a gun linked to a specific crime.

Can researchers get these answers?

What gun shop sold the gun?	No
Who bought the gun?	No
When was the gun traced?	No
How long before the gun ended up in a crime?	No

Instead, the United States goes for smaller laws, fashioned mostly state-by-state. Still, some may be effective. Blocking domestic violence offenders' access to guns seems to cut down on homicides, for example. From 1982 to 2002, states with restraining order laws that bar offenders from buying guns had rates of intimate partner homicide that were 10 percent lower than in states lacking the laws, researchers reported in 2006 in *Evaluation Review*. It's a stark result, and suggests that tough laws can have big impacts. Australia "did an outright ban and something akin to a confiscation of guns," Webster says. "That's never going to happen in the United States."

In 2010, Webster and colleagues reported similar results at the city level. He and colleagues tracked intimate partner homicides from 1979 to 2003 in 46 US cities. Those that made it hard for people with domestic violence restraining orders to get guns had 19 percent fewer intimate partner homicides compared with cities with less stringent laws, the team reported in *Injury Prevention*.

"These are pretty consistent findings," Webster says. Those state policies seem to be working.

Conclusions about other, more well-known laws, such as "right-to-carry," are less convincing. Such laws, which allow people to carry concealed handguns in public, could offer people a means of defense. Or they could make it easier for people in an argument to whip out a gun.

"The findings are all over the map," Hemenway says. A report from the National Research Council in 2005 found no causal link between right-to-carry laws and crime. It also concluded that people do use guns to protect themselves (say, by threatening or shooting an attacker) but how often is hard to say. Estimates vary from 100,000 to 2.5 million times per year in the United States.

Economist Mark Gius of Quinnipiac University in Hamden, Conn., estimated that restricting people's right to carry boosts a state's murder rate by 10 percent, he reported in 2014 in *Applied Economics Letters*.

Donohue's 2014 results lean a different way. The Stanford researcher updated the NRC analysis with more than a decade of new data and found that laws letting people carry concealed weapons boost violent crime—a bit. Based on data from 1979 to 2012, his statistical modeling showed that a state with a right-to-carry law would experience 8 percent more aggravated assaults than a state without such a law, for example.

"More and more evidence is amassing that these laws are harmful," Donohue says, but he concedes that there's still uncertainty. "I'm not quite ready to say that we've nailed it down."

Less uncertainty would require more analyses and more data. But in this field, even that doesn't guarantee consensus.

"The problem is that there are many ways to slice the data," Donohue says. "Almost nothing is as clear as the advocates make it—on both sides."

Print Citations

CMS: Rosen, Meghan. "Gun Research Faces Roadblocks and a Dearth of Data." In *The Reference Shelf: Guns in America*, edited by Betsy Maury, 19-26. Ipswich, MA: H.W. Wilson, 2017.

MLA: Rosen, Meghan. "Gun Research Faces Roadblocks and a Dearth of Data." *The Reference Shelf: Guns in America*. Ed. Betsy Maury. Ipswich: H.W. Wilson, 2017. 19-26. Print.

APA: Rosen, M. (2017). Gun Research Faces Roadblocks and a Dearth of Data. In Betsy Maury (Ed.), *The reference shelf: Guns in America* (pp. 19-26). Ipswich, MA: H.W. Wilson. (Original work published 2016)

The Senate Voted on 4 Popular Gun Control Proposals Monday: Here's Why None of Them Passed

By Amber Phillips
The Washington Post, June 20, 2016

Update: A new poll from CNN shows 92 percent of Americans support expanded background checks and 85 percent support preventing those on terror watch lists from buying guns. As we'll explain in the post below, though, none of the below proposals aimed at these things are likely to pass.

One filibuster, two gun control proposals, four party-line votes, zero compromises, lots of finger pointing.

That's what we can expect Monday evening as the US Senate votes on four different gun control amendments—two offered by Republicans, two by Democrats—a week after the deadliest mass shooting in US history.

We can confidently predict all four of these votes will go nowhere because the Senate took almost the exact same votes in December after the San Bernardino, Calif., attacks. Those votes largely fell—and failed—along party lines, with Republicans supporting looser versions of gun control proposals and Democrats supporting stricter versions.

We have no reason to expect different results Monday. Still, all is not lost: Both sides can and probably will use the results of Monday's votes to rally their bases for November and try and apply pressure to the other side over the next few weeks and months.

Here's a step-by-step guide on what Monday's gun control votes mean and how to follow along.

The ground rules: The votes are expected to start at 5:30 p.m. Eastern time on Monday, and they'll be proposed as amendments to a larger spending bill for the Commerce and Justice departments.

All four amendments will need 60 votes to be included in the package, which will also need to gain final approval. But given the partisan makeup of the Senate (54 Republican, 46 Democrat), and how the gun debate tends to fall neatly along partisan lines, we don't expect any of the proposals to advance.

No. 1: Tighten Up Our Background Check System
(Republican Amendment)

What it proposes: Tries to open the lines of communication between the background check agency that Congress set up in the 1990s, the federal courts, the states and Congress to better carry out background checks. More specifically, defines what it means to be found "mentally incompetent" to buy a gun. Also requires the attorney general to conduct a study on "various sources and causes of mass shootings, including psychological factors, the impact of violent video games, and other factors."

Sponsor: Sen. Chuck Grassley (R-Iowa), chair of the Judiciary Committee

Amendment name to follow along on C-SPAN: S. Amdt. 4751

How this fared in previous votes: Not well. A version of this that Grassley introduced in December failed to clear the 60-vote hurdle, 53-46.

Our prediction: It will fail this time too. Democrats don't think it does enough to expand background checks because, well, it doesn't expand background checks. It simply tries to improve the system we have now.

No. 2: Expand Background Checks (Democratic Amendment)

What it does: Requires that a federal background check be conducted before every gun sale in the U.S., period. (The background check system Congress set up in the '90s only requires background checks by federally licensed firearm dealers, which means you can usually skip it if you try to buy a gun online from a private dealer, at a gun show or from your friend.)

Sponsor: Sen. Chris Murphy (D-Conn.), the senator who talked on the floor for nearly 15 hours Wednesday to demand these votes. (For what it's worth, Senate Republicans say that even before Murphy seized the Senate floor, they expected Democrats to force votes on gun control amendments.)

Amendment name to follow along on C-SPAN: S. Amdt. 4750

How this fared in previous votes: Not well, although it got some bipartisan support. It failed to get the 60 needed to move on, 48-50, although four Republicans voted for it: Mark Kirk of Illinois, Susan Collins of Maine, John McCain of Arizona and Pat Toomey of Pennsylvania.

Our prediction: It will fail again. Most Republicans don't support expanding background checks to gun shows and other purchases—or simply fear any additional gun laws are a slippery slope.

No. 3: Prevent Suspected Terrorists from Buying Guns
(Republican Version)

What it does: Right now, anyone on the FBI's various terrorist watch lists—including the no-fly list that prevents you from getting on a plane—can legally buy a gun. Under this bill, if you're on that list and try to buy a gun, you'd have to wait 72 hours. The idea is to give federal officials time to convince a judge there's probable cause you have ties to terrorism while still protecting the 2nd Amendment rights of anyone who is mistakenly on a terrorist watch list—like the late Sen. Ted Kennedy (D-Mass.) once was. **Sponsor:** Sen. John Cornyn (R-Tex.), Senate Republicans' No. 2 leader

> One filibuster, two gun control proposals, four party-line votes, zero compromises, lots of finger pointing.

Amendment name to follow along on C-SPAN: S. Amdt. 4749

How this fared in previous votes: Not well. (Sensing a trend here?) A similar version failed in December on a 55-44 vote. Democrats—and Attorney General Loretta Lynch—say it's impossible to put together a case that a potential gun purchaser is a suspected terrorist in just three days, so they argue this bill would essentially allow anyone on the watch list to still be able to buy a gun.

Our prediction: It will fail again, for the reasons described above.

No. 4: Prevent Suspected Terrorists from Buying Guns (Democratic Version)

What it does: Lets the attorney general ban anyone on the FBI's various terrorist watch lists from being able to buy guns. If you feel like you're mistakenly on the list and you get denied a gun, you can challenge the FBI's decision in court.

Sponsor: Sen. Dianne Feinstein (D-Calif.)

Amendment name to follow along on C-SPAN: S. Amdt. 4720

How this fared in previous votes: Not well, although it got some bipartisan support. A similar version of this failed in December, 45-54, with two senators voting on the other side: Sen. Heidi Heitkamp (D-N.D.) voted with Republicans against this bill, and Sen. Mark Kirk (R-Ill.) voted with Democrats for this bill.

Our prediction: It will fail again. Republicans think this bill takes away people's constitutional rights for due process because it bans them from buying a gun first, then allows them to challenge it in court later. And even as some Republicans have expressed a willingness to look at the no-fly list proposal—up to and including Donald Trump—they are more likely to favor the GOP proposal over this one.

Some Potential Areas of Compromise

Believe it or not, there are some opportunities—however small—for Congress to move forward on gun control legislation in the wake of Orlando.

For example, here's one new idea that almost all of the four proposals above, have added: If a person who has been on one of the FBI's terrorist watch lists at any point in the past five years tries to buy a gun, the federal government must immediately notify law enforcement about it. The Orlando shooter, Omar Mateen, had been on and off the FBI's watch list before he bought his weapons.

And there are negotiations going on behind the scenes to try to merge Democrats' and Republicans' terrorist watch list proposals. As *The Washington Post*'s

Karoun Demirjian reports, Collins (R-Maine) is working on something that Democrats haven't dismissed outright.

She wants to prevent people on two of the FBI's terrorist watch lists (it's unclear exactly many lists there are for perhaps obvious reasons) from buying guns: the no-fly list and the selectee list.

Both lists deal with a person's rights at the airport. If you're on the no-fly list, you can't board an airplane. If you're on the selectee list, you get extra security screening when you try to board a plane. Mateen was on the selectee list for a time. And under Collins's proposal, if you are on these lists and are denied your right to buy a gun, you can challenge it, and if you win, the government has to pay your legal costs.

Again, her proposals are not exactly what Democrats want (they don't like the idea of working with just these two terrorist watch lists) or what Republicans want (they don't like the idea of banning a person from buying a gun first, then offering legal recourse later). But that's the essence of a compromise, and right now it looks like the only one the Senate's got.

Tellingly, Collins's proposal isn't up for a vote Monday, suggesting it might not yet have backing from Republican leaders.

Update No. 2: All four measures, as expected, failed.

Print Citations

CMS: Phillips, Amber. "The Senate Voted on 4 Popular Gun Control Proposals Monday: Here's Why None of Them Passed." In *The Reference Shelf: Guns in America*, edited by Betsy Maury, 27-30. Ipswich, MA: H.W. Wilson, 2017.

MLA: Phillips, Amber. "The Senate Voted on 4 Popular Gun Control Proposals Monday: Here's Why None of Them Passed." *The Reference Shelf: Guns in America*. Ed. Betsy Maury. Ipswich: H.W. Wilson, 2017. 27-30. Print.

APA: Phillips, A. (2017). The Senate voted on 4 popular gun control proposals Monday: Here's why none of them passed. In Betsy Maury (Ed.), *The reference shelf: Guns in America* (pp. 27-30). Ipswich, MA: H.W. Wilson. (Original work published 2016)

The Gun Fight in Congress

By Jelani Cobb
The New Yorker, July 4, 2016

The House sit-in focused attention on the issue, but more ambitious measures are needed to fix our real gun problem.

On June 14th, Reggina Jefferies, a seventeen-year-old high-school student, attended a vigil in downtown Oakland for two friends who had drowned in a reservoir. As she stood with mourners outside the service, gunfire broke out among a group of men who had been arguing nearby. Four people were wounded; Jefferies was shot dead. The next day, Luis Villot, a twenty-nine-year-old father of four, attempted to defuse a neighborhood dispute at the Farragut Houses, in Brooklyn, and usher some children out of harm's way. When a woman he was trying to calm fired a gun, a bullet struck him in the forehead, and he died three days later. The same day that Villot was shot, Antonio Perkins, a twenty-eight-year-old Chicagoan, was broadcasting a Facebook Live feed of himself talking with people on the street. A car could be seen passing by and returning a few minutes later. Then the screen went black, but the feed captured the sound of gunfire and people screaming. Perkins was shot in the neck and the head, and was pronounced dead that evening.

Last Wednesday, in the same week that Jefferies, Villot, and Perkins were laid to rest, some fifteen Democratic members of the House of Representatives, led by John Lewis, of Georgia, began a sit-in to demand that Congress enact gun-control legislation. (The sit-in lasted nearly twenty-six hours and, eventually, involved a hundred and sixty-eight members.) Barbara Lee, who represents the part of Oakland where Reggina Jefferies was shot, held up a picture of the young woman and said that she had photographs of many more victims of gun violence in her district.

By engaging in a sit-in, a form of protest pioneered during the civil-rights movement, and by having Lewis lead the effort, the Democrats were implying that congressional inaction on gun legislation was, like the federal foot-dragging on segregation fifty years ago, shameful. The sit-in also implied that the people responsible for this state of affairs are as unambiguously wrong as those whom Lewis faced down on the Edmund Pettus Bridge, in Selma, in 1965. Reaction to the sit-in broke along partisan lines. Democratic Senators Chris Murphy, of Connecticut, who had staged a fifteen-hour filibuster to demand action on gun control; Cory Booker, of New Jersey; and Elizabeth Warren, of Massachusetts, walked over to the House chamber to offer their support. (Despite Murphy's efforts, last Monday the Senate blocked several gun measures.) Paul Ryan, the Speaker of the House, denounced the sit-in as "a publicity stunt." It was more substantial than a stunt, though publicity and, more specifically, public pressure were precisely the point of it.

But, from a civil-rights perspective, there were also reasons to be cautious about the proceedings. The Democrats sought to use the example of the shooting of forty-nine people in the Pulse night club, in Orlando, to spur the House to take up legislation that would strengthen background checks and help prevent individuals on the terrorist watch list from purchasing firearms. The argument was that a person deemed too dangerous to fly should be thought of as too dangerous to buy a gun. The

> **The argument was that a person deemed too dangerous to fly should be thought of as too dangerous to buy a gun.**

American Civil Liberties Union, however, announced its opposition to that measure, stating that the list is "error-prone and unreliable, because it uses vague and overbroad criteria and secret evidence to place individuals on blacklists without a meaningful process to correct government error and clear their names." In the current political climate, there is concern that the burden of suspicion will fall disproportionately on Muslim Americans. Beyond that, the proposals wouldn't necessarily have changed the circumstances under which Jefferies, Villot, and Perkins died. Background checks, though important, won't reduce black-market gun sales, the source of the majority of illegal firearms in Oakland, New York, and Chicago.

For the most part, the debate is not about gun violence in America; rather, it's about a narrow variety of spectacular gun violence. The 2012 shooting at the Sandy Hook Elementary School, in Newtown, Connecticut, renewed focus on the availability of assault weapons and their capacity to kill large numbers of people quickly. No significant legislation has passed as a result; by many measures, gun laws have grown looser. The massacres in San Bernardino and Orlando have ignited a push to deny firearms to those who are suspected of terrorist sympathies. Nothing has been done with regard to that, either. But the fact is that mass shootings constitute just two per cent of gun homicides in the United States, and assault weapons are not the weapons most commonly used by Americans to kill one another.

Last year, the Chicago Police Department seized sixty-five hundred and twenty-one illegal firearms. When the Trace, a nonprofit news organization that focuses on guns in America, analyzed the CPD's data, it found that assault weapons were not among the top twenty most frequently used guns. According to the FBI, in 2014 rifles were used in only three per cent of all homicides committed with firearms in the United States. The larger problem, quite simply, is the superabundance of handguns.

The 1994 federal assault-weapons ban, signed by President Bill Clinton, lapsed twelve years ago, and since then the legislation has taken on the aura of a grand achievement, of the sort hardly obtainable in these degraded days. This obscures the fact that it was initially seen as just a first step in gun reform. It prohibited nineteen types of assault weapon but exempted more than six hundred other types of firearm. Current debates about gun reform include proposals for a three-day waiting period; in 1994, advocates pushed for a seven-day waiting period. A ban on cheap handguns that was promoted in 1994 doesn't even enter the discussion now. Our concept of "common sense" gun reform—not to be mistaken for politically viable gun reform—has atrophied even as spectacular violence has become a more constant feature of our lives. "Give us the right to vote on these two bills," Steny Hoyer, the Democratic Whip, implored, from the House floor. "Make America safer!" That statement might more properly be amended to "Make America feel safer."

Compromise legislation, like the bill proposed by Senator Susan Collins, of Maine, which calls for prohibiting people on some watch lists from buying guns, with fail-safes to make the prohibition less random, may yet pass. But it will take much more to diminish the kind of gun violence that claims the greatest number of American lives each year—the kind that killed Reggina Jefferies, Luis Villot, and Antonio Perkins.

Print Citations

CMS: Cobb, Jelani. "The Gun Fight in Congress." In *The Reference Shelf: Guns in America*, edited by Betsy Maury, 31-33. Ipswich, MA: H.W. Wilson, 2017.

MLA: Cobb, Jelani. "The Gun Fight in Congress." *The Reference Shelf: Guns in America*. Ed. Betsy Maury. Ipswich: H.W. Wilson, 2017. 31-33. Print.

APA: Cobb, J. (2017). The gunfight in Congress. In Betsy Maury (Ed.), *The reference shelf: Guns in America* (pp. 31-33). Ipswich, MA: H.W. Wilson. (Original work published 2016)

As Congress Returns, Democrats and Republicans Clash Over Gun Control

By Josh Siegel
The Daily Signal, July 4, 2016

House Republican leaders are planning to hold a vote this week on legislation intended to bar some suspected terrorism suspects from buying guns.

The bill, whose language is backed by the National Rifle Association, is part of an "anti-terrorism" legislative package the House is considering in response to the terrorist attack June 12 at a nightclub in Orlando, Florida.

While Republicans have been reluctant to pursue any legislation that can be construed as gun control, backers of this proposal insist it achieves the delicate balance of preventing those suspected of having terrorist ties from buying weapons— while preserving their right to due process.

"I have not met a single member of Congress who is in favor of terrorists being able to buy guns or explosives," said Rep. Lee Zeldin, R-N.Y., one of the sponsors of the gun measure.

"Unfortunately, Democrats have tried to make it out to be an issue where just one political party is in favor of terrorists not being able to purchase guns or explosives, and that's absurd," Zeldin told *The Daily Signal* in a phone interview on Friday.

"This isn't a debate over whether terrorists should be able to purchase guns or explosives," he added. "This a debate over whether there should be due process for Americans."

After the Orlando massacre, House Democrats staged a sit-in of more than 24 hours demanding action on gun control.

Still, based on early reaction, it appears Democrats won't support the Republican-backed proposal because of concerns that the "probable cause" standard required by the bill is too difficult to achieve.

Senate Democrats have already blocked the same legislation.

"Republicans are again putting the NRA ahead of their responsibility to keep the American people safe," House Minority Leader Nancy Pelosi, D-Calif., said of the Republican proposal in a statement.

One gun-rights group, Gun Owners of America, described the GOP's move as a "cave-in."

The Republican measure, which is based on the language of Zeldin's Protect America Act, would permit the Department of Justice to deny a gun purchase to someone who is being investigated as a known or suspected terrorist, or has been investigated in the last five years.

Law enforcement, however, would have to obtain a court order to prevent a terrorist suspect from buying a gun, and the government would have three business days to prove it has enough evidence of terrorist activity to block the sale.

If the government does successfully prove the suspect "will commit an act of terrorism," the sale is blocked. If it doesn't, the government has to pay the legal costs of the suspect, and the sale can go through.

The suspect is also granted an automatic right to a hearing, and to an attorney.

Democrats believe the three-day window is too short to prove probable cause, arguing the legislation will have little functional impact.

Zeldin counters that the government should have to face a high standard of proof considering the government's terrorist watch lists are controversial. Individuals do not have to be charged with a crime to be placed on the lists, and many don't know they are on them.

> **"I have not met a single member of Congress who is in favor of terrorists being able to buy guns or explosives,"** said @RepLeeZeldin.

"The Department of Justice already knows who these individuals are and already has evidence collected, so the burden should be on the government to demonstrate probable cause that an individual is a terrorist instead of making an American demonstrate that they're not a terrorist," Zeldin said. "That's the way it has always been in our country and the way it should be."

Democrats prefer a bill first introduced in the Senate that would bar guns from being sold to suspected terrorists who are on the FBI's "no-fly" and "selectee" lists.

The House has its own companion version of that bipartisan bill. Under those bills, someone on the no-fly and selectee lists who is blocked from buying a gun can appeal that decision. A court has 14 days to decide on the appeal.

The NRA opposes those bills.

Democrats are framing Republican leadership's decision to bypass a vote on that bill in favor of Zeldin's legislation as the GOP bowing to the NRA. Zeldin tried to downplay the NRA's support of his proposal.

"This isn't the NRA bill," Zeldin said. "Members of Congress wrote this bill, not the NRA. I don't think members should make their determination as to whether or not to vote for or against the bill based on any outside groups support or opposition. It should simply be based on the merit of the proposal and the reality it keeps us safe."

Print Citations

CMS: Siegel, Josh. "As Congress Returns, Democrats and Republicans Clash Over Gun Control." In *The Reference Shelf: Guns in America*, edited by Betsy Maury, 34-35. Ipswich, MA: H.W. Wilson, 2017.

MLA: Siegel, Josh. "As Congress Returns, Democrats and Republicans Clash Over Gun Control." *The Reference Shelf: Guns in America*. Ed. Betsy Maury. Ipswich: H.W. Wilson, 2017. 34-35. Print.

APA: Siegel, J. (2017). As Congress returns, Democrats and Republicans clash over gun control. In Betsy Maury (Ed.), *The reference shelf: Guns in America* (pp. 34-35). Ipswich, MA: H.W. Wilson. (Original work published 2016)

2
Searching for Balance in Gun Policy

A woman holds up a pro gun sign near the site of the Republican National Convention (RNC) in downtown Cleveland on the second day of the convention on July 19, 2016 in Cleveland, Ohio.

Perspectives on Gun Policy

Within the broader ideological debate over gun control/gun rights or personal freedom/collective responsibility, there are a variety of individual issues that have become distinct battlegrounds within the larger discussion, including the debate over assault weapons, the status of current federal restrictions on gun ownership for certain people, and the debate over right-to-carry laws and their effect on crime. In each instance, efforts to pass legislation has been complicated and overly influenced by misinformation and the entrenched attitudes of individuals at the ideological fringes of the debate.

More Dangerous Types of Guns?

One of the central issues involving gun control is the lobby to ban certain types of weapons that gun-control advocates argue are uniquely dangerous. The US courts have supported bans on specific weapons in the past, including the now famous court determination, in the 1939 case of *United States v. Miller,* that ownership of a "sawed-off" or short-barreled shotgun was not protected by the Second Amendment because, in the view of the US Supreme Court, such a weapon was not necessary for self-defense and had no legitimate usefulness in the maintenance of a "well-regulated" militia.[1] Fully automatic weapons, sometimes called "machine guns," have also been prohibited on similar grounds.

In 1994, President Bill Clinton passed the Federal Assault Weapons Ban, banning semi-automatic rifles and pistols typically designed for military use, which lapsed in 2004 when President George W. Bush chose not to renew the ban. As of January 2017, the Supreme Court has refused to hear arguments on state assault weapon laws[2] but the seventh US Circuit Court of Appeals in Chicago upheld an Illinois-state ban on assault weapons in 2016, with Judge Frank Easterbrook, a conservative justice who has supported gun rights, arguing that the court failed to find any justification for the need to allow citizens to own assault weapons for self-defense and that the weapons were uniquely dangerous enough to warrant prohibition.[3] The effort to outlaw assault rifles intensified after the Orlando nightclub shooting of 2016 in which the shooter, Omar Mateen, attacked and killed 49 people at a gay nightclub in Orlando, Florida, using a semiautomatic Sig Sauer MXX rifle that he purchased legally days before the attack.

Writing in *The Federalist*, Sean Davis characterized assault weapons bans as a "stupid idea pushed by stupid people," argued that laws already made it difficult to obtain such weapons, forcing those who wish to purchase them to, in Davis' characterization, "...jump through an obscene number of hoops," and that assault rifles were already prohibitively expensive, suggesting that criminals were too poor to afford them, though this was a challenge that Omar Mateen was apparently able to circumvent.[4] The National Rifle Association (NRA) Institute for Legal Action provides, on its website, ten reasons to oppose assault rifle ban legislation. The reasons provided range from the reasonable argument (reason #4) that assault rifles are used in a relatively insignificant (in comparison to all gun crime) number of deaths, to the far less logical claim (#7) that assault rifle bans will make criminals switch from using assault weapons to concealed weapons. This ignores the fact that the NRA simultaneously favors liberalizing existing restrictions on carrying concealed weapons.[5]

The best argument against banning assault weapons is that assault rifles are not any more dangerous than semiautomatic pistols and therefore that banning assault rifles has little value in deterring violence of crime.[6] In general, polls show waning support for efforts to ban assault weapons, with Gallup reporting an all-time low of 34 percent supporting a complete ban in October of 2016, despite polls indicating that 57 percent supported the ban in June of 2016, in the immediate wake of the Orlando shooting.[7] However, there is no legitimate evidence showing that assault weapons are useful or necessary for self-defense, hunting, or any of the other legitimate uses established by the courts for Second Amendment protection and therefore no legitimate argument against state or federal bans.

More Dangerous Types of People?

Another battleground concerns effort to strengthen laws that prevent former criminals, persons with a history of domestic abuse, and individuals with a history of drug addiction or firearms offenses from purchasing legal guns. Federal laws prohibit persons indicted or convicted of a felony crime (punishable by one year or more imprisonment) from owning a firearm as well as persons who have a history of drug addiction or who have been declared, by judicial authorities, to have mental deficiencies. In addition, persons who have been dishonorably discharged from the military, who have renounced their citizenship, who have been convicted of crimes involving domestic violence (even if misdemeanor crimes) are also prohibited from gun ownership.[8] The federal licensing requirements for individuals selling guns and the federally-mandated background check system are intended to prohibit gun dealers from selling weapons to persons in the above categories. Gun-rights organizations have lobbied against some of the restrictions but the courts have, as of 2017, upheld federal restrictions. There has been a movement, also, to enact legislation making it more difficult for individuals with terrorist ties to purchase weapons, but there is currently no agreement on how the government could effectively legislate such a restriction. Proposals to use the government's Terrorist Watch List as the framework for legislation is problematic and unlikely to be effective.[9]

The American public overwhelmingly supports current federal restrictions and also making federal laws stronger when it comes to legal purchases of firearms.[10,11] However, evidence indicates that current enforcement methods are insufficient. Harvard University's Injury Control Research Center conducted a 2015 study, with a sample size of 2,072 gun owners, indicating that 40 percent obtained guns without having to submit to a federal background check. Currently, only 17 of 50 states require background checks for all gun sales.[12] Despite public opinion on the issue, the weak enforcement practices and lack of consensus on background checks for individuals with links to terrorist organizations has prevented stronger gun-control legislation for these potential gun owners.

The Right-to-Carry Debate

In the late 1990s, conservative academic John Lott published a series of books based on the first (at the time) effort to determine if allowing citizens to carry concealed weapons (known as concealed-carry laws) reduced crime. Critics, before Lott, argued that allowing people to carry guns would lead to an increase in violent gun deaths. Lott's research was controversial from the start, but support for his idea grew through the early 2000s.[13] In 2004, the National Academy of Sciences decided to review all of the available data on concealed-carry permits and crime rates and found that there was insufficient evidence to support Lott's claim that concealed weapons reduce crime, but also that there was insufficient evidence to suggest that the increase in concealed weapons had increased gun violence.[14]

More data on the issue became available over the ten years after the 2004 National Academies study, and the amount of data available increased rapidly as more and more states began allowing citizens to carry concealed weapons. A small number of studies, such as a 2014 study from Stanford University, found that right-to-carry states saw an increase in aggravated gun assaults, by as much as 8 percent, and gun homicides.[15] Coauthor of the study John Donahue has been accused of leftist activism, but the 2014 study was rigorously designed and the statistical models used in the study have statistical and logical merit.

The argument over right-to-carry remains highly contentious, but more and more research has emerged to refute the relationship between right-to-carry and reductions in crime.[16,17] As of 2017 then, data is suggestive, but not conclusive, that right-to-carry and the proliferation of legal guns may increase the likelihood of violent gun deaths and injuries. Current data suggests that earlier studies demonstrating a link between right-to-carry and crime reduction were based on insufficient evidence, or used questionable design, and are therefore insufficient to prove that right-to-carry reduces crime in any capacity. Anecdotal data about individuals with legal guns defending themselves against criminals suggest that, in some cases, this can occur, but do not speak to the broader social effect of right-to-carry policies. Similarly, anecdotal data about persons with legal guns accidentally killing or injuring themselves or others highlight the fact that firearms are dangerous tools, but do not demonstrate that right-to-carry has an overarching effect on the frequency of firearms deaths or injuries. Similarly, data indicating that states prohibiting right-to-carry have higher crime rates (typically focusing on New York, California, New Jersey, etc.) fail to account for population demographics and other factors and so provide no legitimate support for right-to-carry laws.

Micah L. Issitt

Works Used

Barnes, Robert. "Supreme Court Won't Review Laws Banning Assault Weapons." *The Washington Post*. Nash Holdings. Dec 7 2015. Web. 26 Dec 2016.

Beckett, Lois. "The Assault Weapon Myth." *New York Times*. New York Times Company. Sep 12 2014. Web. 27 Dec 2016.

Bialik, Carl. "Most Americans Agree with Obama That More Gun Buyers Should Get Background Checks." *Five Thirty Eight*. Five Thirty Eight. Jan 5 2016. Web. 27 Dec 2016.

"Concealed Carry Permit Holders across the United States." *CPRC*. Crime Prevention Research Center. Jul 9 2014. Web. 27 Dec 2016.

Davis, Sean. "The Assault Weapons Ban Is a Stupid Idea Pushed by Stupid People." *The Federalist*. FDRLST Media. Jun 13 2016. Web. 26 Dec 2016.

"Editorial: What To do about Assault Weapons." *Chicago Tribune*. Jun 14 2016. Web. 26 Dec 2016.

Flowers, Andrew. "The Problem With Using the Terrorist Watch List to Ban Gun Sales." *Five Thirty Eight*. Five Thirty Eight. Jun 20 2016. Web. 27 Dec 2016.

Fortunado, David. "Can Easing Concealed Carry Deter Crime?" *Social Science Quarterly*. 2015. Pdf. 28 Dec 2016.

Grambsch, Patricia. "Regression to the Mean, Murder Rates, and Shall-Issue Laws." *The American Statistician*, Vol. 62, No. 4, 2008, 289-95.

"Identify Prohibited Persons." *ATF*. Bureau of Alcohol Tobacco and Firearms. Sep 22 2016. Web. 27 Dec 2016.

Lott, John R. "Guns and the New York Times: Why Shouldn't Americans Be Able to Defend Themselves?" *Fox News*. Fox News Inc. Feb 24 2015. Web. 26 Dec 2016.

Masters, Kate. "Just How Many People Get Guns without a Background Check? Fast-Tracked Research Is Set to Provide an Answer." *The Trace*. Oct 21 2015. Web. 27 Dec 2016.

"Opinions on Gun Policy and the 2016 Campaign." *Pew Research Center*. Aug 26 2016. Web. 27 Dec 2016.

Parker, Clifton B. "Right-to-carry gun laws linked to increase in violent crime, Stanford research shows." *Stanford News*. Stanford University. Nov 14, 2014. Web.

Swift, Art. "In U.S., Support for Assault Weapons Ban at Record Low." *Gallup*. Gallup, Inc. Oct 26 2016. Web. 27 Dec 2016.

"Ten Reasons Why States Should Reject 'Assault Weapon' and 'Large' Magazine Bans." *NRA-ILA*. Jun 17 2014. Web. 26 Dec 2016.

"*United States v. Miller* 307 US 174 (1939)." *Supreme Justia*. Justia. 2016. Web. 27 Dec 2016.

Wellford, Charles F., Pepper, John V. and Carol V. Petrie. *Firearms and Violence: A Critical Review*. Washington D.C.: The National Academies Press, 2004.

Notes

1. "*United States v. Miller*," *Supreme Justia*.
2. Barnes, "Supreme Court Won't Review Laws Banning Assault Weapons."

3. "Editorial: What To do about Assault Weapons," *Chicago Tribune*.
4. Davis, "The Assault Weapons Ban Is a Stupid Idea Pushed by Stupid People."
5. "Ten Reasons Why States Should Reject 'Assault Weapon' and 'Large' Magazine Bans," *NRA-ILA*.
6. Beckett, "The Assault Weapon Myth."
7. Swift, "In U.S., Support for Assault Weapons Ban at Record Low."
8. "Identify Prohibited Persons," *ATF*.
9. Flowers, "The Problems with Using the Terrorist Watch List to Ban Gun Sales."
10. Bialik, "Most Americans Agree with Obama That More Gun Buyers Should Get Background Checks."
11. "Opinions on Gun Policy and the 2016 Campaign," *Pew Research*.
12. Masters, "Just How Many People Get Guns without a Background Check?"
13. "Concealed Carry Permit Holders across the United States," *CPRC*.
14. Wellford, Pepper, and Petrie, *Firearms and Violence: A Critical Review*.
15. Parker, "Right-to-Carry Gun Laws Linked to Increase in Violent Crime, Stanford Research Shows."
16. Grambsch, "Regression to the Mean, Murder Rates, and Shall-Issue Laws."
17. Fortunato, "Can Easing Concealed Carry Deter Crime?"

A Gun Lover's Case for Gun Control: Not All of Us Believe in the Right to Bear Assault Weapons

By Ron Cooper
Salon.com, June 14, 2016

Extremists are shouting over gun owners like me who favor reasonable restrictions on firearms like the AR-15

I grew up in a family of hunters. My father gave me a .22 rifle and a single-shot .410 shotgun when I was six years old. When my uncles (sometimes an aunt or two) and older cousins got together on a Sunday afternoon, at least one of them had a new gun to show off. The young kids like me were expected to share in the love, and respect, for firearms. I learned about marksmanship, which gun was best for which sort of hunting, that you never use more firepower than is necessary, and most of all, gun safety.

Although I quit hunting years ago (something that most of my relatives found bewildering), I continue to love guns. I like the cool feel of the steel and fruity scent of the oil. I like the hard, metallic clacks of a chamber opening or a clip plunging into place. I like to go to the firing range to squeeze the trigger, receive the recoil, hear the pop, and smell the puff of gunpowder. I like knowing that if an intruder threatens my home, I can protect my family.

I can do all of these things without an assault weapon.

With each tragic mass shooting like the recent one at the Pulse nightclub in Orlando the gun control debate resurrects with renewed vigor. Like most social concerns, the loudest voices tend to be from camps at the opposite poles of the issue's spectrum. One group says that gun ownership is the shank of the problem and calls for severe restrictions on who can own firearms, how many, and what types—the "Guns kill!" camp. The other end sees any restriction as producing a slippery slope that will lead to overturning the Second Amendment—the "They're coming for our guns!" group. The result of such for-me-or-agin-me opposition results in gridlock when legislators consider suggestions for reducing the number of the tragic shooting that keep us all in fear. I believe that the majority of gun owners want reasonable steps, such as banning assault-style weapons, to make our country safer.

The term "assault weapon" is admittedly vague. It usually means a semi-automatic, high capacity gun. An automatic rifle is like a machine gun in that, when you can hold down the trigger, it fires repeatedly and rapidly until you release the trigger. A private citizen cannot lawfully own one of these in some states. A semi-automatic rifle fires as fast as you can pull the trigger. If you can pull it three times per second, it will fire three rounds in that second. High (or large) capacity generally means that the gun can hold more than ten rounds at once. For the AR-15, the

> **No gun owner I have ever known has imagined him- or herself in a situation that called for firing hundreds of rounds within minutes.**

most popular of such guns for private citizens and the weapon of choice for mass shooters, the typical clip holds 30 rounds. Others that hold many more rounds are available. This means that shooter can fire 30 or more rounds without reloading, and for an experienced shooter, an empty clip can be replaced with a full one in a couple of seconds.

Of all the gun enthusiasts that I have known, none has ever owned a weapon with such fire power. Their guns are usually for specific purposes—shotguns and rifles for various sorts of hunting, pistols for home protection, some for target practice only, some of exquisite artistry to hang over the fireplace. No gun owner I have ever known has imagined him- or herself in a situation in that called for firing hundreds of rounds within minutes.

The murderers in mass shootings, however, have imagined themselves doing just that. Since the Federal Assault Weapons Ban (enacted in 1994) expired in 2004, use of these weapons and the numbers of casualties in mass shootings have increased. The shooter in Orlando was first reported to have used an AR-15, which has now been clarified as the Sig Sauer MCX rifle (as the *Washington Post* puts it, "aesthetically similar to and just as lethal as an AR-15"). Shooters in other massacres used similar guns. Think the San Bernardino holiday gathering, think the Aurora, Colorado movie theater, think Umpqua Community College, think Sandy Hook elementary school. Other mass shooters used high-capacity pistols, such as the Virginia Tech shooter's Glock 19 whose 15-round clip is standard.

I am familiar with the "They're coming for our guns" group's reasons for opposing a ban on assault weapons.

Guns don't kill people; people kill people. Of course this platitude is true, but people can kill far more people in a shorter amount of time with assault weapons. These guns are designed to cause great destruction as they have done too many times.

Banning assault weapons will not keep them out of a determined person's hands. Again, this may be true, but should we make it easy for them? Besides, automatic weapons, such as machine guns, are heavily restricted and illegal in many states. The mass shooters have not used them but have instead chosen the legally and easily obtained semi-automatic weapons.

A trained gunman can kill just as many people with any other sort of gun. The evidence from mass shootings speaks otherwise. According to research from Everytown for Gun Safety, based on data from the FBI, in mass shootings from January 2009 to July 2015, when high-capacity magazines were used, 155 percent more people were shot and 47 percent more people died.

If we let them ban assault weapons, they'll take away our Second Amendment rights altogether. This is the worst sort of slippery-slope argument, one that ignores obvious distinctions. (I'll bracket the discussion of whether the clumsily-worded Second Amendment is about private ownership or a "well regulated militia" only, for the Supreme Court has ruled that the amendment guarantees private ownership rights.) Most people, including gun owners, of course, are capable of making distinctions among different sorts of weapons. This alarm assumes that we can see no difference between an AR-15 and a .38 revolver. Here in Florida, as in other states, I cannot own a ballistic knife (one that ejects a detachable, spring-powered blade). That ban has not affected my carrying a pocket knife or wearing a sheath knife.

A bumper sticker on my truck reads "Gun Toting Liberal." Several times I've had people lower their car windows at traffic lights to comment on the apparent oxymoron. I am an enigma to my liberal friends who do not own guns and are in the "Guns kill!" camp. I befuddle my conservative friends who do not own guns but nevertheless side with the "They're coming for our guns!" bunch. But for my gun-owning friends across the political spectrum, gun ownership is not a partisan issue. Similarly, we have more agreement than not regarding restrictions on what sorts of firearms should be illegal. I hope that these people and others like them, the ordinary gun owners of America, will speak up and be heard over the extremists who have blocked reasonable discussion of legislation concerning assault weapons.

Print Citations

CMS: Cooper, Ron. "A Gun Lover's Case for Gun Control: Not All of Us Believe in the Right to Bear Assault Weapons." In *The Reference Shelf: Guns in America*, edited by Betsy Maury, 45-47. Ipswich, MA: H.W. Wilson, 2017.

MLA: Cooper, Ron. "A Gun Lover's Case for Gun Control: Not All of Us Believe in the Right to Bear Assault Weapons." *The Reference Shelf: Guns in America*. Ed. Betsy Maury. Ipswich: H.W. Wilson, 2017. 45-47. Print.

APA: Cooper, R. (2017). A gun lover's case for gun control: Not all of us believe in the right to bear assault weapons. In Betsy Maury (Ed.), *The reference shelf: Guns in America* (pp. 45-47). Ipswich, MA: H.W. Wilson. (Original work published 2016)

How I Got Licensed to Carry a Concealed Gun in 32 States by Barely Trying

By Tim Murphy
Mother Jones, September/October 2013

I was clueless, hung over, and totally worthless with a firearm. Four hours later, I was officially qualified to pack heat.

According to the state of Utah, I earned the right to carry a concealed handgun on a Saturday morning in a suburban shopping center outside Baltimore. Toward the back, next to a pawnshop and White Trash Matt's tattoo parlor, is the global headquarters of Dukes Defense World, a mom-and-pop firearms instruction shop certified by the Utah Bureau of Criminal Identification to teach nonresidents firearm safety as a prerequisite for obtaining a concealed-carry permit.

My achievement doesn't make sense for a number of reasons. One, I don't live in Utah. I'm a resident of Washington, DC, a city that holds concealed handguns in roughly the same esteem as working escalators. I've never shot a gun. And in distinctly un-Utahn fashion, I'm nursing a hangover. Fortunately, none of that matters here. After four hours at Dukes Defense, I have a completed application and a snazzy graduation certificate for my wall. Sixty days after my application is processed, I'll be able to carry a concealed weapon in no fewer than 32 states. It's great for road trips.

Over the last two decades, Utah's concealed-carry permit has emerged as a de facto national ID for handgun owners. It typifies a new era of arming Americans in public: 40 states now recognize some or all out-of-state permits, and 8 have made it legal in all or some circumstances to carry a concealed handgun without any permit at all. In April, the Senate came just three votes short of passing a measure that would have mandated reciprocity for concealed-carry permits—including the ones Utah so freely hands out—nationwide.

As part of a National Rifle Association-backed movement to roll back concealed-carry restrictions, in the mid-1990s Utah became a "shall issue" state. That means it grants concealed-carry permits unless it has a compelling reason (such as a felony record) not to do so. Licensees don't need to demonstrate proficiency with a handgun, and they don't even need to set foot in the Beehive State. They just have to take a class on firearm safety and pay a processing fee (approximately $50) and some of the cheapest renewal fees in the business (as little as 75 cents every five years).

The result has been a boom in out-of-state residents seeking permits and the birth of a cottage industry catering to them. As of June, nonresidents held more than 60 percent of Utah's 473,476 valid concealed-carry permits. Maryland alone has 33 Utah-certified instructors. One, Mid-Atlantic Firearms Training, boasts "No Firearm Qualification Needed"; another, Semper Fidelis Consulting, touts its NRA ties and its convenience. (It makes house calls.)

My instructor is Kevin Dukes, a 20-year Army veteran who runs Dukes Defense World with his wife, Jenny. He's ready for battle in cargo pants, a black polo, hiking boots, and black-rimmed hipster glasses that match his gray goatee. A handgun is on his hip. A black-and-white portrait of shotgun-pumping Hatfields—icons of responsible gun ownership if ever there were—sits in the corner. Across the room is a table with a paper invitation that will be his first topic of discussion: "Join the NRA."

The pitch is straightforward. It costs just $35 to sign on with America's top gun lobbying group, and membership comes with $2,500 of insurance in case anything happens to your piece. Dukes concedes that not everyone is a fan of the NRA's politics, but in his view the group puts together smart training programs and its aim is true—"320 million people a year are being saved by guns, because they're not being killed," he tells us.

Dukes' presentation focuses mostly on the law, or lack thereof, in Utah. He walks us through the verbal warnings we should give before using lethal force, but ends with a caveat: "In Utah, you're not obligated to do that. You don't have to do the hokey pokey and then turn yourself around." In 1994, Utah was one of the first states to adopt a so-called Stand Your Ground law, the expansive self-defense doctrine now on the books in dozens of states and made famous after George Zimmerman killed Trayvon Martin.

We listen to a 911 call from a Utah woman whose husband had just killed a home invader. Dukes asks us what we'd do in that situation, and one of my classmates, who has already committed to moving to Texas to escape Maryland's gun-grabbing government, says immediately that she'd pull the trigger. Dukes' lesson: If you're not prepared to kill, you're not prepared to carry.

Gun rights activists boast that issuing more concealed-carry permits drives down crime and protects even non-gun-owners. But claims about millions of annual "defensive gun uses" are not backed up by reliable data. What statistics there are indicate that enforcement is marred by racial disparity: A white person who shoots a black person is 11 times more likely to have the homicide classified as justifiable than in the reverse situation, according to an analysis by the Urban Institute. (*Mother Jones'* ongoing investigation of public mass shootings shows that 5 of the 23 shootings that occurred since 2010 were carried out by killers using legally concealed handguns.)

While only 9 states had shall-issue laws on the books in 1980, today 41 do—great news not only for the likes of Dukes Defense, but also for the $12 billion gun manufacturing business. As a top NRA lobbyist noted in describing her work on concealed carry in 1996, "The gun industry should send me a basket of fruit." Gun makers have taken to advertising directly to permit holders: Kahr Arms boasts that

"Nothing fits better undercover" than its PM9 handgun. An ad for North American Arms' mini-revolver touts that "NO gun is easier to carry or conceal."

There has also been a push to conceal the growing numbers of people carrying weapons to church or the mall. In just the first five months of this year, 16 states passed a total of 33 laws relaxing concealed-carry restrictions, not only making guns permissible in more public places, but also sealing off permit records. West Virginia went so far as to exempt concealed-carry permit holders from federal background checks when purchasing firearms.

Utah lawmakers' latest idea is to eliminate the requirement for a permit within the state's borders entirely—what's known as "constitutional carry." In March, Republican Gov. Gary Herbert vetoed such a bill, but gun lobbyists are planning to make another push. Constitutional-carry-type laws already exist in eight

> **"The gun industry should send me a basket of fruit,"** said a top NRA lobbyist who pushed for concealed-carry laws.

states, including Arizona, where former Rep. Gabby Giffords' assailant was exercising his legal right to carry a Glock 19 and high-capacity magazines. When I asked Carrick Cook, a spokesman for the Arizona Department of Public Safety, what it takes to carry a concealed handgun in Arizona, his response was brief: "Pretty much nothing." (Residents in constitutional-carry jurisdictions may need to get a permit if they want to cross state lines with a weapon, but that's usually a formality.)

As Dukes walks us through a long list of precautions, it's clear that he's passionate about safety. It's equally clear that I don't know the first thing about how to responsibly handle a firearm, let alone carry one in public. Jenny invites us to come up front to practice loading a handgun with fake rounds. When my turn comes, I struggle to load more than a few before they're ejected halfway across the room. But that's not going to stop Utah from giving me a permit.

A few weeks after my graduation, I call up Dukes. My application is still being processed, but a question has been nagging at me: What did a seasoned instructor think about the fact that pretty much anyone could walk in and get a Utah permit without demonstrating a lick of proficiency with a gun? While he seems disappointed that I signed up for the class with no actual desire to protect myself, he hardly hesitates: "The Constitution doesn't say you need it."

Print Citations

CMS: Murphy, Tim. "How I Got Licensed to Carry a Concealed Gun in 32 States by Barely Trying." In *The Reference Shelf: Guns in America*, edited by Betsy Maury, 48-50. Ipswich, MA: H.W. Wilson, 2017.

MLA: Murphy, Tim. "How I Got Licensed to Carry a Concealed Gun in 32 States by Barely Trying." *The Reference Shelf: Guns in America*. Ed. Betsy Maury. Ipswich: H.W. Wilson, 2017. 48-50. Print.

APA: Murphy, T. (2017). How I got licensed to carry a concealed gun in 32 states by barely trying. In Betsy Maury (Ed.), *The reference shelf: Guns in America* (pp. 48-50). Ipswich, MA: H.W. Wilson. (Original work published 2013)

It's Time to Ban Guns. Yes, All of Them

By Phoebe Maltz Bovy
The New Republic, December 10, 2015

Ban guns. All guns. Get rid of guns in homes, and on the streets, and, as much as possible, on police. Not just because of San Bernardino, or whichever mass shooting may pop up next, but also not *not* because of those. Don't sort the population into those who might do something evil or foolish or self-destructive with a gun and those who surely will not. As if this could be known—as if it could be assessed without massively violating civil liberties and stigmatizing the mentally ill. Ban guns! Not just gun violence. Not just certain guns. Not just already-technically-illegal guns. All of them.

I used to refer to my position on this issue as being in favor of gun control. Which is true, except that "gun control" at its most radical still tends to refer to bans on *certain* weapons and closing loopholes. The recent *New York Times* front-page editorial, as much as it infuriated some, was still too tentative. "Certain kinds of weapons, like the slightly modified combat rifles used in California, and certain kinds of ammunition, must be outlawed for civilian ownership," the paper argued, making the case for "reasonable regulation," nothing more. Even the rare ban-guns arguments involve prefacing and hedging and disclaimers. "We shouldn't 'take them away' from people who currently own them, necessarily," writes Hollis Phelps in Salon. Oh, but we should.

I say this not to win some sort of ideological purity contest, but because *banning guns* urgently needs to become a rhetorical and conceptual possibility. The national conversation needs to shift from one extreme—an acceptance, ranging from complacent to enthusiastic, of an individual right to own guns—to another, which requires people who are not politicians to speak their minds. And this will only happen if the Americans who are quietly convinced that guns are terrible speak out.

Their wariness, as far as I can tell, comes from two issues: a readiness to accept the Second Amendment as a refutation, and a reluctance to impose "elite" culture on parts of the country where guns are popular. (There are other reasons as well, not least a fear of getting shot.) And there's the extent to which it's just so *ingrained* that banning guns is impossible, legislatively and pragmatically, which dramatically weakens the anti-gun position.

The first issue shouldn't be so complicated. It doesn't take specialized expertise in constitutional law to understand that current US gun law gets its parameters from Supreme Court interpretations of the Second Amendment. But it's right there in the First Amendment that we don't have to simply nod along with what follows. That the Second Amendment has been liberally interpreted doesn't prevent any of us from saying it's been misinterpreted, or that it should be repealed.

When you find yourself assuming that everyone who has a more nuanced (or just pro-gun) argument is simply better read on the topic, remember that opponents of abortion aren't wondering whether they should have a more nuanced view of abortion because of *Roe v. Wade*. They're not keeping their opinions to themselves until they've got a term paper's worth of material proving that they've studied the relevant case law.

Then there is the privilege argument. If you grew up somewhere in America where gun culture wasn't a thing (as is my situation; I'm an American living in Canada), or even just in a family that would have never considered gun ownership, you'll probably be accused of looking down your nose at gun culture. As if gun ownership were simply a cultural tradition to be respected, and not, you know, about *owning guns*. Guns... I mean, must it really be spelled out what's different? It's absurd to reduce an anti-gun position to a snooty aesthetic preference.

> **That the Second Amendment has been liberally interpreted doesn't prevent any of us from saying it's been misinterpreted, or that it should be repealed.**

There's also a more progressive version of this argument, and a more contrarian one, which involves suggesting that an anti-gun position is racist, because crackdowns on guns are criminal-justice interventions. Progressives who might have been able to brush off accusations of anti-rural-white classism may have a tougher time confronting arguments about the disparate impact gun control policies can have on marginalized communities.

These, however, are criticisms of certain tentative, insufficient gun control measures—the ones that would leave small-town white families with legally-acquired guns well enough alone, allowing them to shoot themselves or one another and to let their guns enter the general population.

Ban Guns, meanwhile, is not discriminatory in this way. It's not about dividing society into "good" and "bad" gun owners. It's about placing gun ownership *itself* in the "bad" category. It's worth adding that the anti-gun position is ultimately about police not carrying guns, either. That could never happen, right? Well, certainly not if we keep on insisting on its impossibility.

Ask yourself this: Is the pro-gun side concerned with how *it* comes across? More to the point: Does the fact that someone opposes gun control demonstrate that they're culturally sensitive to the concerns of small-town whites, as well as deeply committed to fighting police brutality against blacks nationwide? I'm going to go with *no* and *no* on these. (The NRA exists!)

On the pro-gun-control side of things, there's far too much timidity. What's needed to stop all gun violence is a vocal *ban guns* contingent. Getting bogged down in discussions of what's feasible keeps what needs to happen—*no more guns*—from entering the realm of possibility. Public opinion needs to shift. The no-guns stance needs to be an identifiable place on the spectrum, embraced unapologetically, if it's to be reckoned with.

Print Citations

CMS: Bovy, Phoebe Maltz. "It's Time to Ban Guns. Yes, All of Them." In *The Reference Shelf: Guns in America*, edited by Betsy Maury, 52-54. Ipswich, MA: H.W. Wilson, 2017.

MLA: Bovy, Phoebe Maltz. "It's Time to Ban Guns. Yes, All of Them." *The Reference Shelf: Guns in America*. Ed. Betsy Maury. Ipswich: H.W. Wilson, 2017. 52-54. Print.

APA: Bovy, P.-M. (2017). It's time to ban guns. Yes, all of them. In Betsy Maury (Ed.), *The reference shelf: Guns in America* (pp. 52-54). Ipswich, MA: H.W. Wilson. (Original work published 2015)

The Gun Control "Terror Gap": What Is It— and Why Hasn't Congress Fixed It?

By Andrew Gumbel
The Guardian, June 16, 2016

In the wake of the Orlando attack, Republicans have expressed a willingness to compromise on the purchase of guns by people on terrorist watch lists but legislation is still far from a certainty. Here's why:

Democrats ended a 14-hour filibuster in the Senate overnight with the promise of some progress on proposed gun control legislation. Republicans leaders agreed to take a vote on amendments to expand background checks and ban gun sales to those who are on the government's terror watch list, closing what is known as the "terror gap".

It's unknown how Republicans would vote on the proposals. But in the wake of the nightclub shootings in Orlando, a small handful of them in the Senate are now showing greater willingness to compromise on the terror proposal than they did last December, when rival measures from the two parties to close the terror gap in the wake of the San Bernardino shooting both failed.

Meanwhile, Donald Trump, the presumptive Republican nominee for the White House, is scheduled to talk to the NRA on Thursday to help formulate his own policy position on the so-called terror gap—a not-so-subtle acknowledgement of the extraordinary power that the gun lobby wields over legislators and candidates for high office alike. Here's what you need to know about the terror gap.

What Is the Terror Gap?

The terror gap is the notion of a legislative hole whereby US citizens can purchase deadly firearms even if they are under investigation for suspected terrorist activity. The Government Accountability Office found that between 2004 and 2014, some 91% of suspected terrorists who attempted to buy a gun—2,043 out of 2,233—succeeded.

Attempts to close the gap, going back to the George W Bush administration, have repeatedly failed despite broad public support because of pressure on congressional legislators from the NRA.

Is This Another Case of Partisan Gridlock?

Not entirely. The Bush and Obama administrations have both supported the same set of proposals, and the legislation most hotly contested by the NRA has been proposed jointly by Dianne Feinstein of California, a Democratic senator, and Peter King of New York, a Republican congressman. That said, Republicans tend to be in lockstep with the NRA more consistently than Democrats. Fifty-four senators voted against the Feinstein-King legislation last December, 53 of whom were Republicans. Just one Republican, Mark Kirk of Illinois, voted in favor.

The FBI has different ways of categorizing people it is investigating for possible terrorist ties. In addition, there is a federal no-fly list of people deemed too dangerous to be allowed to board an airplane. Some in the Senate, including Republican Pat Toomey, want to create a single consolidated list and have it subject to the authority of the foreign intelligence surveillance, or FISA, court.

> **The terror gap is the notion of a legislative hole whereby US citizens can purchase deadly firearms even if they are under investigation for suspected terrorist activity.**

What Are the Ideas for Fixing It?

Feinstein and King want to give the Department of Justice, which includes the FBI, sole discretion over which terrorist suspects get to purchase weapons and which do not—in part so that the FBI has the option of allowing sales to go ahead as part of their investigative process. Anyone who feels unfairly targeted would still have a chance to appeal against any denial of gun rights in the courts.

The NRA's preferred approach, currently championed in the Senate by Republican John Cornyn, would require the government to respond to a contested gun sale by filing a brief in federal court, offering the targeted individual the opportunity to make his or her case in response, and convincing the judge to rule within 72 hours. Without fulfilling all of these conditions, the sale would go ahead. The president of Michael Bloomberg's group Everytown for Gun Safety said this week: "The Cornyn bill has an absurdly high standard that applies only to people who are proven to be about to commit a terrorist act. At that point, we shouldn't be debating about terrorists' gun rights—just about the quickest way to incapacitate them."

Among those seeking a compromise is Toomey, a Republican facing re-election in Pennsylvania, a key swing state. He wants to address concerns about government overreach leading to people being put on a list erroneously by consolidating the many different ways the FBI has of tracking terror suspects, as well as the federal no-fly list, and putting it under the authority of the FISA court.

If Closing the Terror Gap Is So Popular, What Is the Argument Against It?

Detractors on the left and the right are worried that a list of terror suspects used to curtail individual liberties would be prone to abuse and inadequate constitutional safeguards. The no-fly list has come under fire for exactly this criticism. Many people have not been informed that they are on the list, making it difficult or impossible to get themselves removed, and many others have not been given a reason for their inclusion. The American Civil Liberties Union is engaged in a five-year-old legal battle to challenge the constitutionality of the no-fly list and would accept it as a basis for denying individual gun rights only "with major reforms".

The NRA, for its part, cites the risk of governmental overreach as a cornerstone of its argument for subjecting any contested gun purchase to the scrutiny of a judge. In principle, the NRA says it wants to keep guns out of the hands of criminals and terrorists, but in practice it has set almost impossibly high bars to making this happen.

If the Terror Gap Had Been Closed, Would It Have Prevented the Massacre in Orlando?

Probably not. The Feinstein-King legislation as written last December would not have covered Omar Mateen because the FBI twice put him on a list of suspected terrorists and then took him off again. They now have new language, tailored to the events in Orlando, to extend a weapons purchase ban for five years after an individual is put on a terrorism suspect list.

Of course, there are many other ways to obtain an assault rifle and a machine pistol such as the weapons used at the Pulse nightclub than by going into a gun store – for example, at a gun show, where there are no background checks. Another bill that will now go up for a vote to require background checks at gun shows is much less likely to pass.

Are the Chances of Closing the Gap Now Any Greater Than They Were After Any of the Other Recent Atrocities?

Slightly, but don't hold your breath. Senators such as Toomey and Rob Portman of Ohio, also facing re-election this year, are indicating an interest in finding compromise language. Feinstein, however, said on Wednesday that her own efforts to find a middle ground were not working. "I don't think it's going to work out," she said.

Why Is Trump Talking to the NRA Before Announcing His Own Position on the Issue?

Because, as Ari Freilich, a staff attorney with the Law Center to Prevent Gun Violence, put it: "The NRA sets the term of the debate." That applies even to a presidential candidate who famously claims to be beholden to nobody. The NRA has endorsed Trump, and Trump is doing what many, many other NRA endorsees have done before him.

Print Citations

CMS: Gumbel, Andrew. "The Gun Control 'Terror Gap': What Is It—and Why Hasn't Congress Fixed It?" In *The Reference Shelf: Guns in America*, edited by Betsy Maury, 55-57. Ipswich, MA: H.W. Wilson, 2017.

MLA: Gumbel, Andrew. "The Gun Control 'Terror Gap': What Is It—and Why Hasn't Congress Fixed It?" *The Reference Shelf: Guns in America*. Ed. Betsy Maury. Ipswich: H.W. Wilson, 2017. 55-57. Print.

APA: Gumbel, A. (2017). The gun control "terror gap": What is it—and why hasn't Congress fixed it? In Betsy Maury (Ed.), *The reference shelf: Guns in America* (pp. 55-57). Ipswich, MA: H.W. Wilson. (Original work published 2016)

Anti-Gun Hysteria Is Hazardous to Your Health

By David French
National Review, December 5, 2016

The data prove it. Despite their avowed faith in science and data, all too many progressives view a gun as a kind of magical, evil object. It's a metallic voodoo doll that is best not touched, handled, or brought into polite conversation, even when it can save lives. I remember one of the last briefings I received in my Army career. A military police major stood in front of roughly 100 soldiers and clicked through PowerPoint slides describing how service members and their families could protect themselves from terrorist violence. Slides described suggestion after suggestion as to how to conceal your identity as an American soldier and render your movements unpredictable. It was good advice, but something was missing.

At the conclusion of the briefing, I raised my hand and asked why the Pentagon wasn't recommending that its soldiers—as a group the most highly trained warriors in the country—legally carry a personal weapon off-post. The response was instant: "Because the data indicate you're more likely to hurt yourself than harm a criminal." A murmur went through the room. I followed up. "Do you carry a weapon off-post?" He looked sheepish, but confessed. "Yes I do. At all times." I thought of that moment while reading David Montgomery's lengthy essay in the most recent *Washington Post Magazine*. Montgomery's piece is a powerful meditation on life in an era where more people and institutions than ever before must ponder how to respond to mass shootings. It walks through the emerging consensus that "run, hide, and fight" is best policy—that first you should try to escape an attacker, and, if that doesn't work, your best and only option is to fight back. Montgomery details what this means: "As a last resort, we must convert our fear into anger. We must swarm the attacker, swinging laptops, coffee mugs, scissors." Laptops? Coffee mugs? It all seems so hopeless.

But don't tell the *New York Times*. Last week it editorialized against legislation that would require states to recognize lawful concealed-carry permits issued in other states. In "support" of its argument, it tried to make the case that permit holders are a threat to public safety. Using research from the anti-gun Violence Policy Center, it ominously claims that "since 2007, concealed-carry permit holders have been responsible for at least 898 deaths not involving self-defense." Follow the link to the study, called "Concealed Carry Killers," and you'll find that almost 300 of those 898 deaths were suicides. Where does that number fit within the context of all gun deaths in the United States? During the same ten-year span when 898 deaths occurred, there were more than 100,000 homicides and more than 300,000 total gun deaths. Given that approximately 6 percent of the adult population has a concealed-carry permit, legally concealed weapons are involved in remarkably few deaths. Simply put, if you're standing at a bus stop, and you know the person to your left is an armed concealed-carry permit holder, and the person to your right does not have a carry permit, the person to your right is statistically a far, far greater threat to your life than the permit holder. That's just a fact. Indeed, that person's hands and feet are more dangerous to you than the permit holder's gun. Applying the *New York Times*'s own preferred data set, more people were murdered by fists and kicks in 2015 alone than were murdered by firearm-wielding concealed-carry permit holders in the last ten years.

Given that most of us will never face an active shooter, his rise to prominence is more about us than him. He's the perfect nightmare, an avatar of the minute-to-minute possibility of terrorism ripping the facade off the familiar. Can we do what it takes to be ready without letting him haunt our lives? I feel like raising my hand again. Yes, yes there is something you can do. You can arm yourself. When you do, you no longer feel helpless because you're not. You don't have to rely on your laptop or a pair of scissors to save your life and the lives of those around you. You can walk into a restaurant, a mall, or any other place where firearms are permitted with confidence, not as a vigilante, but as an armed citizen capable of defending yourself and others. Yet anti-gun hysteria too often triumphs over common sense. Bring up expanded concealed-carry rights, and some on the Left seem to panic as if law-abiding men and women will somehow turn our shops and schools into free-fire zones. But the evidence is overwhelming: Concealed-carry permit holders are not a public-safety risk. In July, the Crime Prevention Research Center published a comprehensive report on those Americans who hold concealed-carry permits. Among the findings, the Center notes that while the police are dramatically more law-abiding than the population as a whole (37 times more law-abiding), permit holders in Texas and Florida—two states that keep comprehensive records—were even more law-abiding than cops. Police officers committed crimes at a rate of 103 crimes per 100,000 officers. Permit holders in Texas and Florida committed crimes at a rate of 22.3 per 100,000.

This means that those opposed to concealed carry on campuses and those supporting so-called gun-free zones in other public spaces are behaving irrationally. Those who are training law-abiding citizens to respond to mass shootings without also counseling them to purchase a firearm and learn how to use it aren't empowering their clients as much as they could. (I don't want to cast too much blame; often the clients don't want to be empowered.) America has a crime problem. It doesn't have a gun problem. The gun is a tool, not a terror. In the right hands, it's an instrument of peace and justice. It protects life and stops attacks. It's an antidote to fear and helplessness. We cannot allow hysteria to prevent us from exercising our inherent right of self-defense.

Print Citations

CMS: French, David. "Anti-Gun Hysteria Is Hazardous to Your Health." In *The Reference Shelf: Guns in America*, edited by Betsy Maury, 59-60. Ipswich, MA: H.W. Wilson, 2017.

MLA: French, David. "Anti-Gun Hysteria Is Hazardous to Your Health." *The Reference Shelf: Guns in America*. Ed. Betsy Maury. Ipswich: H.W. Wilson, 2017. 59-60. Print.

APA: French, D. (2017). Anti-gun hysteria is hazardous to your health. In Betsy Maury (Ed.), *The reference shelf: Guns in America* (pp. 59-60). Ipswich, MA: H.W. Wilson. (Original work published 2016)

Four Major Problems with Gun Control Arguments

By Dustin Murphy
The Federalist, June 21, 2016

Every mass shooting and act of terror is an opportunity for liberals to push gun control. Something must be done to stop gun violence, but there are four problems with the liberal argument for gun control. These are: (1) hypocrisy; (2) reality; (3) misapplication of blame; and (4) discrimination. In the end, there is a better, more reasonable solution.

1. Gun Control Hypocrisy

Gun control contains three types of hypocrisy. The first is the contradiction of protection (value of human life), the second is the contradiction of solution (terrorism and criminals), and the third is the contradiction of right-control.

The argument for gun control is, essentially: human life is valuable, killing humans is wrong, guns kill humans, so, limit access to guns to protect human life. Liberals' wish to protect human life, however, does not apply to everyone, since under their policies some life is not valuable, like those of the preborn.

House Minority Leader Nancy Pelosi said whether a baby in the womb is human doesn't have anything to do with policy. To win over pro-abortion women, Hillary Clinton said the Constitution does not protect the unborn. Liberal policy is to ignore the value of some life to advance a perceived "right" to attain votes.

When society arbitrarily dictates which life has value, it does two things: (1) fosters a culture where not all human life has value, so some humans can be discarded or treated less than others, to the point of killing them; and (2) says humans can arbitrarily decide which human life has value. So, aborting some (preborn) is warranted and morally acceptable because they do not have value, while aborting others (born) is unwarranted and immoral because they have value.

It's contradictory to argue that access to an instrument (guns) should be limited because a class of people (born) have value, but simultaneously that access to other instruments (vacuum, uterine currette, syringe, embryotomy scissors, Dubois embryotomy decapitating scissors) should not be limited because a class of people (preborn) have no value.

The second problem is the contradiction of solutions. The liberal answer for defeating violent extremism (i.e., radical Islamic terrorism) is jobs and social programs. Vice President Joe Biden, at a three-day White House summit on terrorism, opened by stating societies must provide economic alternatives to terrorism. Marie Harf, a spokeswoman for the State Department, told Chris Mathews on "Hardball" that we must counter terrorism by providing job opportunities. In February 2015, President Obama's framework for fighting violent extremism was education, jobs, and social programs. So if the root cause of violence and the solution to violent extremism overseas is job opportunities, education, and social programs, it should be the political solution to violence in America. Not gun control.

Third, liberals ensure Americans that government control of guns is not a restriction on Second-Amendment rights. This is a contradiction in right-control.

When Hillary spoke this year at the Hartford Connecticut YMCA, she said that as president she would change the "gun culture," and could do this consistent with the Second Amendment. Liberals wouldn't tolerate language like, "As president I would change the death culture, controlling abortion consistent with the Fourteenth Amendment," or, "As president I would change discrimination toward women by limiting access to pornography." When some states or organizations want to change the "death culture" or "porn culture" consistent with the Fourteenth or First Amendments, liberals accuse them of sending America back to the Stone Age, and Planned Parenthood or the ACLU sues.

2. Gun Control Doesn't Respond to Reality

Some want to turn what's illegal into a right (e.g., drugs, prostitution, or illegal immigration) or argue that decriminalizing certain things (e.g., drugs or prostitution) lessens crimes. About guns, however, the argument is the opposite. Either it's viewed as a "right" not to protect or argued that criminalizing it would lessen crimes.

Making guns illegal or restricting access to them won't end gun violence. By analogy, possession and use of many controlled substances is illegal, yet people possess and use them. Indeed, illegal drug overdose is the leading cause of death in America (a study released by the Drug Enforcement Agency found that overdose death is the leading cause of injury death in the United States, over vehicles and firearms).

Obama has used Australia and England as lofty examples of Western societies ending gun violence. However, depending on the study cited, there is no clear and convincing evidence that gun homicides in Australia have declined since the ban on certain weapons and their buyback plan (National Firearms Agreement). Studies do agree that suicide rates have declined.

The Associated Press, though, says criminologists agree the National Firearms Agreement has reduced gun homicides. Results following England's self-proclaimed "toughest gun control laws in the world" are known and are not good; crimes using banned weapons have risen. At a glance, gun control in Australia (which doesn't have a Bill of Rights), seems to have decreased gun violence; yet, it depends on the studies. In reality, however, prohibiting an act or an object does not necessarily reduce crime or violence.

3. Gun Control Misapplies Blame

Journalists and many politicians blame guns, mental illness, or some other thing when a shooting occurs. Although mental illness could be a contributing factor, it is not the cause. After Columbine, the media also blamed Marilyn Manson. Manson's response was two-fold: (1) times have not become more violent, just more televised and (2) the blame for the shootings is not music but us: "When it comes down to who's to blame for the high school murders in Littleton, Colorado, throw a rock and you'll hit someone who's guilty."

> **Gun control proponents are full of hypocrisy, don't tailor their demands to reality, misapply blame, and use law to discriminate.**

Violence is not something new to this world. Before guns there was violence and mass killings. What has changed is the mass production of violence and its glamorization. Movies and video games romanticize violence or make it grotesque, desensitizing the conscious and natural disdain towards it. When the heart becomes numb to violence and taught to act on passions, a violent reaction will occur when someone decides to act. As Jesus said, it is not what is put into the mouth that defiles a man, but what comes out of the heart. Blame falls not on the instrument, but on us as individuals for defiling our hearts.

4. Gun Control Is Discriminatory

The Contradiction of Protection above leads to discrimination. Advocating for laws to protect one group while disregarding the rights of another is discrimination. A country having gone through a Civil War that nearly ripped it apart once treated blacks as property and women as second-class citizens. It still treats babies and women as property and babies as second-class. It is discrimination to say Germans should live but not Jews, whites should live but not blacks, the born should live but not the preborn.

It's a utilitarian worldview centered on the self to discriminately apply the Constitution or natural rights on only certain groups so the majority within a protected class can live in harmony. Selfishness of rights breeds violence. We think ourselves advanced, caring, and tolerant, but still foster discrimination and violence towards certain groups when advocating for laws that protect one class over another. Advocating for gun control while advocating for abortion and pornography is utilitarian selfishness, based on the premise that the preborn and women can be discriminated against while appearing altruistic.

What We Should Do Instead

First, foster a culture of respect for all human life, from conception to natural death. Also, in response to mass shootings, the response should be focused on the shooter's depraved heart and the religion or philosophy that drives him, not on the instrument used to kill. Individuals must start to control what comes into the heart, and society must root itself in virtue, the Commandments, the Beatitudes, and spirituality.

School education needs to include moral and ethical principles founded on the natural law. Last, offering free classes on firearm safety will teach responsible use of firearms, decreasing its glamorization. Wars and crimes will never be eradicated, but violence can be substantially reduced.

Print Citations

CMS: Murphy, Dustin. "4 Major Problems with Gun Control Arguments." In *The Reference Shelf: Guns in America*, edited by Betsy Maury, 62-65. Ipswich, MA: H.W. Wilson, 2017.

MLA: Murphy, Dustin. "4 Major Problems with Gun Control Arguments." *The Reference Shelf: Guns in America*. Ed. Betsy Maury. Ipswich: H.W. Wilson, 2017. 62-65. Print.

APA: Murphy, D. (2017). 4 major problems with gun control arguments. In Betsy Maury (Ed.), *The reference shelf: Guns in America* (pp. 62-65). Ipswich, MA: H.W. Wilson. (Original work published 2016)

Inside the Power of the NRA

By Robert Draper

The New York Times, December 12, 2013

To get to Joe Manchin's private office in the Hart Senate Office Building, you first pass through a lobby where you encounter a small bronze statue of an Old West law-man holding a firearm—an award given to Manchin several years ago by a chapter of the National Rifle Association for his unswerving defense of gun rights. Then you turn down a hallway, past several framed photographs of children who were victims of the massacre a year ago at Sandy Hook Elementary School in Newtown, Connecticut. The combination of the bronze rifleman in the lobby and the young faces on the wall suggests a particular viewpoint—*I stand with gun lovers; I stand with victims of gun violence*—that qualifies, in Washington anyway, as being nuanced, which is to say politically ill advised if not suicidal.

Even sitting behind his stately wooden desk in a suit and tie, Manchin, who is 66, possesses the craggy appearance of a small-town sheriff. As he proclaimed to me one morning in September, "I enjoy my guns, and my family enjoys their guns." And indeed, Manchin, a conservative Democrat from West Virginia, won election to the U.S. Senate in 2010 partly on the strength of a memorable TV ad depicting him firing a bullet through President Obama's cap-and-trade bill that had been anathema to coal miners in his state. But Manchin's outlook changed the day he came back from a hunting trip last December, having learned of the 20 children and six adults slaughtered at Sandy Hook. That unique horror motivated him in a way that other recent mass shootings in Tucson and Aurora, Colorado, had not.

"To sit here and do nothing, I could've done that all day long," Manchin said. "Let this be the happy retirement home." Instead, for the first time in his 30-year political career, he acted against the NRA's wishes. He introduced legislation that would require universal background checks for commercial sales. Background checks have been federally mandated for firearm purchases from licensed dealers since 1994. The bill would have extended them to gun shows and all Internet sales. Manchin was aware that universal background checks would not have prevented the Newtown killings, because the shooter, Adam Lanza, used firearms that were legally purchased by his mother. Nonetheless, a confluence of factors at the time favored his efforts: a newly re-elected Democratic president personally stung by the gun tragedies that took place on his watch; a fractious and self-doubting Republican Party; the seemingly bottomless financial resources of the New York mayor and ardent gun-control advocate Michael Bloomberg, whose alliance of more than a thousand mayors throughout the United States, Mayors Against Illegal Guns, would sponsor an aggressive wave of TV ads; and the forceful but sympathetic lobbying presence of Gabrielle Giffords, the former congresswoman who had been shot in the head in Tucson, along with the voices of the Newtown parents whose children were killed. Given this climate and the overwhelming public support for universal background checks, even the NRA was braced for the passage of some version of Manchin's gun-control bill. But no version did pass. Four months after the Newtown shooting, on April 17, the bill failed to win the necessary votes to make it through the Senate. The most fearsome lobbying organization in America prevailed once again. Other victories would soon follow. On the day before I visited Manchin's office in September, two state senators who spearheaded a recent passage of tough gun-control legislation in Colorado were recalled—another triumph for the NRA, despite having been outspent by Bloomberg's group. (A third Colorado state senator who supported the bill announced her retirement last month in the face of a recall.) Not long after that, a mentally unhinged gunman at the Washington Navy Yard, less than two miles from the Senate office buildings, killed 12 employees. In his eulogy for the victims, the president noted somberly: "Once more our hearts are broken. Once more we ask why." But few were asking why Joe Manchin or some other senator wasn't out trying to round up more votes for his bill. If the murder of 20 schoolchildren had proved insufficient motivation to address gun violence in America, this killing was not enough to persuade anyone to take on the NRA again.

"As far as putting on a full-court press, I don't see that happening," Manchin told me in his office. "And I don't hear much conversation about it." The defeat of the bill has added to the legend of the gun lobby's brawn. Though the NRA's opponents still question whether the group is really as indomitable as it is perceived, at a certain point, political mythology engineers its own reality. One recently retired congressman from a conservative district told me, "That was the one group where I said, 'As long as I'm in office, I'm not bucking the NRA.'"

Still, a year after the Newtown killings, the question of why nothing new has been done to address America's gun violence is a vexing one. To begin to answer it requires a close look at why Joe Manchin failed in his effort to pass a fairly minimal change—closing loopholes in the existing gun laws. The defeat of the bill not only provides a case study in how the NRA operates but also reveals its potential frailties. Whether the NRA's new and well-financed adversaries can exploit them is another matter. Doing so will most likely involve more than just standing up for the vulnerable young faces on Manchin's wall. It will also require taking stock of, and appreciating, the resonance of the armed figure in his lobby.

President Obama was at his desk on the afternoon of the Newtown shootings, when two speechwriters, Jon Favreau and Cody Keenan, entered the Oval Office to receive his edits of the statement they wrote about the horrendous episode. "I can't read that," Obama said quietly, crossing out a couple of lines. "I won't be able to get through them."

That evening, Obama convened a group of top aides in the Oval Office and informed them that passing gun legislation would now take priority in his already-cluttered second-term agenda. Five days later, at a news conference, Obama announced that Vice President Joe Biden would be leading a monthlong search for "proposals that I then intend to push without delay." When a reporter asked, "What about the NRA?" the president replied: "Well, the NRA is an organization that has members who are mothers and fathers. And I would expect that they've been impacted by this as well. And hopefully they'll do some self-reflection."

The NRA was doing precisely that. In the week that followed the shooting, the organization's two top officials—its chief executive, Wayne LaPierre, and Chris Cox, the executive director of the NRA's Institute for Legislative Action—spoke by phone numerous times. LaPierre, who is 64, was paid a salary of $831,709 in 2011, according to federal tax returns. He spends the majority of his time on the road, raising money and interacting with NRA members, who routinely address him by his first name. Despite his accessibility with gun owners and the homespun manner in which NRA phone solicitors tell members that "Wayne" would like to offer them discounts on NRA products, LaPierre is notably guarded with the media. After Newtown, he traveled with security guards who, because of death threats, cased TV studios in advance of his rare interviews. (The NRA refused my repeated requests to speak with him.) By contrast, Cox, who is 43, is the group's inside man whose office is a short walk from the Capitol in a small space above Bullfeathers, a popular watering hole for Hill staff members.

In their conversations, Cox told LaPierre that he did not yet have a clear sense of how their congressional allies were reacting to the Newtown shootings. Cox's instinct was that the NRA should stay quiet for the time being, as it had done following past shootings. Instead LaPierre decided to respond forcefully, without consulting the NRA's lobbyists or its full 76-member executive board. One week after the shootings, he stood behind a lectern at the Willard InterContinental hotel a few blocks from the White House and broke into a blistering attack on the news media, the movie industry and video-game manufacturers while defiantly declaring, "The only thing that stops a bad guy with a gun is a good guy with a gun." Several NRA-friendly legislators found LaPierre's speech to be tone deaf and recommended to his colleagues that someone else serve as the group's spokesman.

LaPierre's combativeness was nonetheless in keeping with the NRA's recent history as an organization that views its cause as an embattled one. It hasn't always been that way. Founded in 1871 to teach marksmanship to city-dwelling Union soldiers, the group was originally a nonpolitical and noncontroversial league of sportsmen and remained so for nearly a century. Everything changed, however, during the urban tumult of the 1960s, culminating in the assassinations of Martin Luther King Jr. and Robert Kennedy. The 1968 Gun Control Act imposed a licensing system for purchases, mandated serial numbers on weapons, banned certain gun imports and barred felons and illicit drug users from obtaining firearms. Gun-loving legislators like Representative John Dingell of Michigan worried that even harsher restrictions were imminent and clamored for the NRA to wake up and enter the political arena.

The lobbying arm, the Institute for Legislative Action, was formed in 1975. Two years later at a now-famous annual convention in Cincinnati, Dingell and other NRA allies ousted the group's reigning executives, who saw the organization largely as a haven for gentlemen hunters, and replaced them with fire-breathing Second Amendment absolutists. The new lobbying director, Harlon Carter, then led an energetic campaign to boost membership. "Harlon came up with the idea that they'd need four million members, and everybody thought this was impossible, but by golly, he did it," Dingell told me. (Today the NRA claims that it has more than five million dues-paying members, though there is reason to believe that this figure is at least somewhat inflated. Millions more do not pay dues but—perhaps because they've taken the group's firearm-safety course—say in surveys that they are members.)

The NRA scored its first major victory when Dingell and other friends on the Hill succeeded in passing the Firearm Owners' Protection Act of 1986, which restored many of the gun rights that were outlawed by the 1968 law. Once the Democrats regained the White House in 1993, the NRA was again put on the defensive, when President Bill Clinton and Congress passed a ban on assault weapons. The gun group then targeted the bill's proponents during the midterm elections. Many of them lost and Republicans became the majority. "The NRA is the reason Republicans control the House," Clinton ruefully observed, thereby cementing the group's reputation as a political force to be feared.

Following the Columbine shootings in 1999, in which some of the weapons used were bought at gun shows, Clinton pushed for universal background checks. Initially, the NRA went on record supporting an amendment by Dingell that watered down a bill extending background checks to gun shows. But ultimately the scandal-ridden and lame-duck president was no match for the NRA, whose congressional allies killed the bill entirely. By the time the Virginia Tech murders occurred in 2007, it was a fact of life in Washington: Any major legislation that the NRA opposed stood little to no chance of passage.

But the uniquely awful nature of the Newtown tragedy, coupled with Obama's recent victory, augured a battle far more difficult than any the NRA recently faced. Aware that the struggle would be fierce and expensive, the group made it "as easy as we could for people to join," says David Keene, who recently retired as NRA president. It offered discounts on annual and lifetime memberships. In the six months after Newtown, as gun-control advocates pushed for legislation, the NRA was able to recruit more than a million new members, Andrew Arulanandam, an NRA spokesman, said. This meant millions more for the group's coffers.

Still, the gun lobby had no clear sense initially of how its efforts would be waged, and to what end. On January 10, 2013, Biden hosted a meeting in his Executive Office Building suite with several Second Amendment supporters, including the veteran NRA lobbyist Jim Baker. When Biden asked if the NRA would consider supporting a ban on assault weapons or high-capacity magazine clips, Baker's answer was a crisp "no." But when asked the same thing about universal background checks, Baker equivocated, saying, "I'd have to see what you're talking about."

Baker knew this was thorny territory for the NRA Extending background checks to firearms purchases at gun shows and over the Internet, with the aim of making it harder for felons and the mentally ill to acquire weapons, remains popular and not just among liberals. According to a CBS News/New York Times poll taken in the days after the Biden meeting, 92 percent of Americans favored universal background checks. A poll conducted by the Republican pollster Frank Luntz indicated that there was 74 percent approval among self-identified NRA members—in keeping with the 77 percent approval in a survey of hunters commissioned by the Bull Moose Sportsmen's Alliance. (The NRA dismisses these high numbers but has offered none of its own. Three days after the Biden meeting, the Republican polling firm OnMessage conducted a survey for the NRA of its members on a variety of legislative topics—but was not instructed to ask about universal background checks.) After Newtown, the NRA lobbyists suspected that if the Democrats were to reintroduce Dingell's 1999 background-checks bill, there would be no political will to oppose it.

In January, Biden's task force announced its legislative recommendations. These included universal background checks, a ban on assault weapons and limits on magazine capacity. Each initiative would successfully pass through the Senate Judiciary Committee, whose chairman was Patrick Leahy—himself an owner of more than a dozen firearms who has spent time during Vermont winters shooting at large chunks of ice. Though it was clear from the outset that there would never be enough votes in the Senate to pass either an assault-weapons ban or a limit on magazine capacity, progressives were convinced that their moment had arrived on universal background checks. During one meeting between several Democratic senators and some of the Newtown parents in early February, Al Franken of Minnesota openly conveyed the optimism many on his side of the issue were feeling. "There's not an argument— there aren't two sides to this," he said, according to someone who was present. "This is common sense. And that's the end of it."

Not every Democrat felt so sanguine. Any bill that made it out of the Senate would face stiff opposition from the Republican-controlled House. Other pressing issues (like immigration) loomed on the legislative calendar, and the Senate majority leader, Harry Reid, had no desire to see the agenda overtaken by gun control. Like Leahy, Reid was a gun owner who was keenly aware of the place firearms hold in American life—and who recognized that not everyone in his party understood this. At roughly the same time that Franken and other Democratic senators were plotting their legislative strategy, their Democratic counterparts in the House met for an annual retreat in Leesburg, Va. Among the gathering's main events was a seminar on how to talk to voters about firearms and gun legislation. But not one of the four panelists—a Yale law professor, a political reporter, a former Orlando police chief who ran for Congress on the Democratic ticket and the veteran Beltway strategist Anita Dunn—could claim a true appreciation of American gun culture. According to two attendees, when Dunn was describing the desirability of background checks, she used the word "registration"—thereby conjuring up the specter of a national registry of all licensed guns, a notion that is abhorrent to many gun owners, who fear that registering firearms with a federal agency would make it easier for the government to one day confiscate them. "She kept using the R-word," one attendee recalls. "And what I took away was that nobody in the Democratic Party knows how to talk about this."

Joe Manchin shared the concern that the Democrats who were leading the charge on gun legislation didn't understand how deeply people care about guns and needed to if they were ever to get anything passed. By January the universal background-checks legislation was being spearheaded in the Senate by Charles Schumer, a liberal from New York City. "Joe, I didn't know anybody who owned a gun when I grew up," Schumer said to Manchin, who replied, "Chuck, I didn't know anybody who *didn't* own a gun." Schumer's bill contained no provisions that might attract the support of gun owners, a fatal omission in Manchin's view. "The bill Chuck Schumer dropped was one that I didn't think anyone from a gun state would or should support," Manchin told me. "So I reached out to the NRA and said, 'Let's have an alternative.'"

In early March, Chris Cox and Jim Baker came to Manchin's office to hear him out—the first of several face-to-face meetings they would have that month. Manchin knew that the lobbyists were never going to embrace universal background checks. His hope was simply that they would not fight him. To win their neutrality, Manchin had all sorts of ideas for an NRA-friendly bill. In his version, firearms dealers would, for the first time since 1968, be allowed to sell handguns across state lines, including at out-of-state gun shows. Members of the military and their spouses could purchase guns in their native state and in the state where they were stationed. Such provisions had been championed by the gun group for years. "I told the NRA, 'When will you ever have a time when liberals who hate us even having a gun actually vote for something that protects and enhances our rights—and all we ask for in return is to tighten up loopholes in legislation that's already there?' " he said. "Absolutely, I said that to them. Many, many times."

Among the NRA's most-activist members, however, there is a powerful suspicion that one restriction will open the door to more, each new limit leading inexorably to a time when there will no longer be a right to bear arms. Throughout March, the NRA employed the familiar mechanics of lobbying the dozen or so senators—including Democrats facing tough re-election battles in 2014 like Mary Landrieu of Louisiana and blue-state Republicans like Kelly Ayotte of New Hampshire—who had not yet decided whether they would support the bill. They pressed for face time with the senators, cozied up to their aides and urged NRA members in their states to harangue the Washington offices. Cox and Baker were aware that the senators were also feeling pressure from the White House and gun-safety groups—and, of course, from Joe Manchin, a fellow NRA member and sportsman who actively sought to allay the fears of red-state legislators that his bill would be impossible to sell back home. Recognizing, for example, that a chief talking point of the gun lobby was that universal background checks might enable a government agency to compile a national registry, he added a section that would make the attempt to do so punishable by a 15-year prison sentence. By early April, Manchin found a willing

Republican co-sponsor: Pat Toomey of Pennsylvania, the former president of the fiscally hawkish Club for Growth who, like Manchin, had received an A rating from the NRA (Toomey hailed from a blue state and, says someone closely involved in the legislative strategy, "he needed something to show to more moderate voters in Pennsylvania that he's not an ideologue.")

For the time being, then, Cox and Baker's only recourse was to make Manchin's bill as attractive to gun owners as possible, in the event that it became law. Through email and phone calls, NRA lobbyists inundated Manchin's office with suggested bill changes. Among these were small but meaningful technicalities like refining the legal definition of "gun show" and exempting certain firearm purchases from background checks. When the Manchin-Toomey bill was officially made public on April 10, the language included numerous provisions that were explicitly, according to someone involved in the negotiations, "NRA ask-fors."

The NRA prefers quashing a bill it doesn't like or pushing a favored bill through Congress with traditional arm twisting. But if it can't do that, the organization strives to be in the room while legislation is being hashed out; and once there, it will cut deals with any ally it can find, including Democrats. This is the way of all lobbying organizations, of course. As David Keene, the former NRA president, put it: "Our effectiveness is totally dependent on the fact that we reward our friends, and we stand with them. Our goal isn't to elect Republicans. It's to support people who support the Second Amendment." The NRA declared war on those who helped pass the 1994 assault-weapons ban, most of whom were Democrats, but while the bill was being crafted, the NRA worked with two of its House Democratic allies, John Dingell and Jack Brooks of Texas, to weaken it so that if it did pass, it would apply to only a limited number of firearms and would expire a decade later. (It did not pass again.) Following the Virginia Tech shootings in 2007, the NRA skillfully aligned itself with both the Brady Campaign to Prevent Gun Violence and Carolyn McCarthy, a New York congresswoman and ardent gun-control advocate, to pass legislation that would improve the flow of state mental-health and criminal records to the F.B.I. database.

But a handful of smaller, more strident gun groups—most notably the Gun Owners of America and the National Association for Gun Rights—have continually attacked the NRA for giving any ground, for negotiating with the enemy and, worst of all, for helping to elect lukewarm allies. By way of defending the organization's strategy, Keene says: "The difference between the NRA and a lot of these other gun

> By the spring of 2013 it had become axiomatic in the Senate that among the three incendiary social issues of the moment—gun restrictions, same-sex marriage and comprehensive immigration reform—a moderate Democrat could afford to vote for two of them, and a conservative Republican only one.

organizations is that it's easy enough to stand and say, 'You shouldn't compromise on anything.' Our job is to actually get things done."

Still, getting things done requires compromise, which is frowned upon by the group's hard-core base. This dilemma has plagued the NRA since it achieved passage of the 1986 Firearm Owners' Protection Act, an NRA triumph that came at a cost: to garner enough votes among Democrats, Wayne LaPierre, who then led the NRA's federal lobbying effort, agreed to a provision in the bill that banned the future sale of machine guns. Richard Feldman, an NRA lobbyist back then and now its critic, said: "At the time, there was a huge controversy among the activist groups about the NRA being a sellout. 'They gave away your rights on machine guns!' This was long before an Internet. Now it would be all over the place, and people would question what the NRA did."

That kind of instant, frenetic backlash is precisely what occurred during the spring of 2013, when word began to leak out that the NRA's top lobbyists were once again in the back room discussing gun legislation. On March 25, Dudley Brown, executive vice president of the National Association for Gun Rights, sent a mass email to thousands of gun enthusiasts that began: "It's happening. . . . According to Politico, Sen. Joe Manchin is in secret negotiations with unnamed NRA officials to sell out our gun rights. I've warned you from the beginning that our gravest danger was an inside-Washington driven deal." In the email, Brown damningly referred to the deal as "the Manchin-NRA compromise bill."

A week later, on April 1, about 250,000 gun-rights sympathizers received an email from the Gun Owners of America, which promotes itself as "the only no-compromise gun lobby in Washington." The email warned, "The media has been reporting that the NRA is working" with Manchin. It concluded, "If you are an NRA member, contact them," and helpfully supplied the NRA phone number, directing recipients to address their grievances to Wayne LaPierre.

The Gun Owners of America and the National Association for Gun Rights each has less than a tenth of the NRA's reported five million members and each has only one full-time lobbyist (the NRA has more than a half-dozen federal lobbyists alone). Yet, as two people connected to the NRA acknowledged to me, extreme gun groups can influence the NRA simply by casting it as the establishment organization, much as Tea Party candidates have pushed mainstream Republican incumbents farther to the right. That would seem to be what occurred in the case of the Manchin-Toomey bill. For it was immediately following pressure from the hard-liners that the NRA lobbyists suddenly and without notice backed away from the background-checks bill.

A few days after the Gun Owners of America's mass email, Cox and Baker stopped communicating with Manchin's office. (The NRA denies that its withdrawal from the process was a result of pressure from other gun groups.) On the afternoon of Monday, April 15, Manchin was surprised to learn about an email that the NRA had sent to his Senate colleagues. The email (a similar version of which went out to NRA members) ended any pretense of neutrality by announcing that the organization would vehemently oppose the Manchin-Toomey bill. In addition, the organization said it would "score" the vote—meaning, it would factor into its election-year grading system how each senator voted on the bill. (In some conservative states, an NRA grade can be determinative; as one former legislator told me, "When you come from a state like mine, you'd better be with them 100 percent.")

Aghast, Manchin got Jim Baker on the phone. "Jim, why'd you change?" he recalls asking.

Rather than answer the question, Baker simply replied: "We're totally opposed to it. We're going to be fighting it with all we have."

The phones soon began to ring throughout Senate office buildings, jamming up the lines in front offices and rolling over into those on many staff members' desks. In Pat Toomey's office, the calls ran nine to one against the bill. In Manchin's office, the ratio was 200 to one in opposition, with many citing the fear that the bill would lead to a national registry despite the provision that explicitly made it a felony to do so. The NRA enlisted the aid of a paid phone-calling organization to mobilize its members by forwarding willing participants directly to their senators' phones. Regardless of what prompted the calls, what Senate staff members heard was the distinct and fevered outcry of a single-issue constituency with every intention of echoing its wrath at the ballot box. This was the NRA's base in action.

Manchin stepped up his personal lobbying. He and his other allies, like Gabby Giffords and her husband, Mark Kelly, quickly recognized that the gun bill wasn't being viewed in isolation. Sometimes that worked in their favor. While visiting their Arizona friend John McCain, Giffords and Kelly were two minutes into their pitch on the background-checks bill when McCain interrupted them: "Oh, yeah, yeah, of course. I'm with you. Now, immigration? I'm going to need *your* help."

But for several other undecided senators, the gun bill constituted one political burden too many. This was evident during a meeting between Rob Portman, who is a Republican senator from Ohio, and several parents of the slain Newtown children. Portman told them, "You know, I have an A rating from the NRA, so I'm probably not going to support this." At some point, 13-year-old James Barden, a brother of one of the victims, spoke up. "Senator, there's over a thousand deaths from gun violence in Ohio every year," he said. "I'm here on behalf of my little brother, Daniel. Do you think that this bill would save some of those lives?"

Portman sat quietly for a moment. Then he said: "It could. It could." But what the Republican senator did not say was that he had already disappointed conservatives by coming out in favor of same-sex marriage because of his openly gay son. By the spring of 2013 it had become axiomatic in the Senate that among the three incendiary social issues of the moment—gun restrictions, same-sex marriage and comprehensive immigration reform—a moderate Democrat could afford to vote for two of them, and a conservative Republican only one. Portman had already selected his hot-button issue.

Harry Reid scheduled the vote on the Manchin-Toomey bill for Wednesday, April 17. The previous weekend, Manchin, Toomey and Schumer divvied up the list of undecideds whom they needed to call. Democrats had been hopeful that Toomey could bring as many as 10 Republicans on board. Thus far, none would commit.

Manchin was having problems of his own with the undecided Democrats. Max Baucus crossed the NRA back in 1994 by voting for the assault-weapons ban and, a former Baucus staff member told me, he "felt he had paid dearly for that" in the form of attack ads and wrathful constituents. Baucus was viewed as a near-certain no. Mark Pryor of Arkansas faces a tough re-election in 2014; he was also aware that his father, Senator David Pryor, like Baucus, voted for the 1994 assault-weapons ban and incurred the animus of the NRA Heidi Heitkamp of North Dakota had just begun her first term after defeating a Republican who received the NRA's endorsement. The flood of calls from Heitkamp's new constituents registered roughly seven to one against the background-checks bill.

By late Sunday, Manchin, Toomey and Schumer glumly compared notes. The weekend calls failed to produce a single new vote in favor of the bill. Then, on the afternoon of Monday, April 15, explosive devices went off at the Boston Marathon. That evening, while mayhem dominated the news coverage, one of the key swing senators in the gun debate, Jeff Flake of Arizona, posted on his Facebook page that he intended to vote no.

The following afternoon, Flake was in a Capitol Visitor Center restroom before heading to a conference room that was about to be dedicated to Gabe Zimmerman, the former staff member of Gabby Giffords who was killed by the Tucson gunman. Inside, the senator encountered a fellow Arizonan who was also heading to the dedication: Giffords's husband Mark Kelly.

Kelly pulled a copy of the Manchin-Toomey bill out of his pocket. He wanted to know specifically what Flake's objections were. The two began to debate the wording of individual sentences. As Kelly would later tell me, he thought that Flake's tortured reasoning—combined with the fact that the NRA spent more than $345,000 on his Senate race last year—seemed like evidence "that he was trying to get to 'no.'"

Flake stepped out of the men's room. Shortly afterward, Gabby Giffords met them by the door. The former congresswoman—whose speaking skills remain badly impaired since being shot in the head—fixed Flake with a glare of anger and disappointment.

But Flake's decision to vote no began the cascade. On Wednesday, Joe Manchin stood on the floor of the Senate as the votes stacked up against his bill. In the end, the final tally was 54 to 46 in favor of the bill. But that was not enough to reach the 60-vote threshold the bill required and the legislation was defeated. Afterward, several senators came up to shake Manchin's hand and express kind words for his political courage and determination. Half-listening, Manchin scanned the gallery, where he knew some of the Newtown parents were sitting. In a few minutes he broke away and gathered the families in an anteroom. He managed to stare into their eyes and assure them that he was far from done. Their children's faces were on his wall, and he would not forget them.

"Harry Reid told me that as soon as I've got 60 votes, he'll bring it to the floor for a vote," Manchin said in his office recently. But his tone suggested that this was not something anyone should expect anytime soon. As to what legislative compromises would be needed to swing the necessary votes his way while not alienating the ones he already had—and then, to find Republican supporters in the House—Manchin could only say he was open to whatever ideas his colleagues might have.

Yet even as the votes in the chambers still favor the NRA, gun-control advocates have some cause for optimism. Time does not seem to be on the NRA's side. According to data compiled by the nonpartisan National Opinion Research Center, between 1977 and 2012 the percentage of American households possessing one or more guns declined by 36 percent. That decline should not be surprising. Tom W. Smith, director of the research center, says: "There are two main reasons, if you ask people, why they have firearms: hunting and personal protection. Now, from external sources like the federal Fish and Wildlife Service, we know the proportion of adults who hunt has declined over the decades. And since the '90s, the crime rate has fallen. So the two main reasons people might want to have a gun have both decreased."

The NRA is all too aware of the headwinds it faces and has ramped up its efforts. In recent years, it has targeted young military veterans by offering them a free introductory "Life of Duty" membership. It also works extensively with the Boy Scouts, David Keene told me, "to try to get kids in the city to hunt and fish." The NRA's signature method of recruitment, however, is to play on the fears of gun enthusiasts with over-the-top claims that President Obama and his administration will not rest "until they've banned, confiscated and destroyed our guns, just like they did in England and Australia." Over time, this tactic could prove to be a losing one. Just as Tea Party rhetoric has hurt the Republican Party among young people and Hispanics, the NRA's seeming capitulation to the smaller, no-compromise gun groups risks turning off whole swaths of mainstream gun owners who may be more concerned with the job market and the cost of college tuition than with the prospect of a national gun registry.

For now, the matter of universal background checks joins immigration reform and same-sex marriage as issues in which Washington Republicans lag behind nationwide public opinion. And so the more competitive gun-legislation battles have begun to take place at the state level. Following the shootings in Newtown, tighter gun restrictions have passed in 20 states, including Connecticut, New York, Delaware, Illinois and Colorado, while a ballot-initiative effort is under way in Washington State to pass a background-checks bill that was defeated in the Legislature earlier this year. Meanwhile, 27 states have loosened, in some manner, gun laws that were already on the books. Some states did both.

"The NRA has had this issue to itself for a generation," Mark Glaze, the executive director of the Bloomberg-backed Mayors Against Illegal Guns, said, referring to the NRA's dominance of an overmatched gun-control lobby. On the subject of the Manchin-Toomey defeat, he said: "Would we have done anything differently? We might have started advertising sooner and more broadly. We might have paid millions rather than thousands of dollars to ship telephone calls into offices. But it's entirely possible that none of that would've made a difference, because you're at the early stage of a process that has several stages."

If part of this early stage is figuring out how to exploit the NRA's vulnerabilities, Glaze and others must also face up to why it is that the NRA has continued to beat them soundly and far more consistently than the Republicans have defeated Democrats—namely, by motivating its supporters to make themselves heard in a way that gun-control adherents haven't. One gun-control group that seeks to close the intensity gap is Moms Demand Action, which was started by Shannon Watts, a 42-year-old Indiana-based public-relations veteran and mother of five, the day after the Newtown shootings. "I think what's been missing are the voices of mothers," Watts told me. Most gun-control organizations "have been run by men," she said. "Women are the caretakers of the family, and the ones who make most of the spending decisions. Most of us don't realize—I certainly didn't—that it's easier to buy ammunition than Sudafed. But the massacre of innocent children in the sanctity of their schools woke us up."

Though underfinanced, Watts's group (which, she says, consists of 125,000 volunteers nationwide) has staged attention-getting Stroller Jams—rallies of women with strollers at state capitols and congressional offices—and pressured Starbucks to request that customers not bring firearms into its stores. More often than not, Watts told me, men with semiautomatic weapons slung over their shoulders show up to her group's events, and she routinely receives vile phone messages and threats against her and her children.

While Moms Demand Action employs confrontational tactics, Gabby Giffords and Mark Kelly have opted for a more soothing approach. Following the defeat of the background-checks bill, Giffords and Kelly, co-founders of Americans for Responsible Solutions, have spent much of their time touring rural regions and meeting with gun owners. "We're trying to make it a habit to engage with folks who don't think we're on the same side of the issue," Kelly told me the day after he and Giffords visited a gun show in upstate New York. "More than anything, they just want to be listened to—and to hear that we know something about where they're coming from. Hell, I'm as much of a supporter of the Second Amendment as Wayne LaPierre. I'd far rather spend my day at a gun show than at an antique show."

But the point behind this blue-collar diplomacy, Kelly told me, is to build consensus on addressing a painful conundrum: "It's been almost a year since 20 schoolchildren were massacred, and so far our national response has been to do nothing."

"Washington, D.C., is a difficult place to get things done," Nicole Hockley said with arch understatement when I visited her in Newtown one morning recently. The first time I met her, two weeks after the defeat of the background-checks bill and less than five months after the death of her son Dylan, Hockley seemed freighted with a bottomless fatigue. Though grief was hardly behind her, she now appeared more buoyant and intent on rising above the legislative mire. Recently, Hockley said, she spent several days attending focus groups of gun owners in Memphis, Phoenix and Chicago. Sitting in a dark room and peering through one-way glass, she listened as people who looked and sounded very much like her spoke of their love for their children and their affection for their firearms. It struck her, she told me, that "only one out of more than 60 didn't support background checks."

Hockley also recently met with a firearms instructor to learn more about the Bushmaster semiautomatic rifle that Adam Lanza used to kill her son. She said she has a "perverse need" to come to terms with the weapon used to shoot Dylan, as part of a larger attempt to understand gun culture. Her effort represents a way of doing individually what those in the gun-control movement might need to do collectively—break down the barriers of fear and mistrust from which the NRA derives much of its power.

As the instructor spoke, she stared at the weapon and listened intently. He asked her whether she would like to shoot it or at least hold it. Hockley shook her head. "This is as far as I can go today," she told the instructor with tears in her eyes. And that was the way these things would have to progress, in unsteady little increments.

Print Citations

CMS: Draper, Robert. "Inside the Power of the NRA." In *The Reference Shelf: Guns in America*, edited by Betsy Maury, 66-78. Ipswich, MA: H.W. Wilson, 2017.

MLA: Draper, Robert. "Inside the Power of the NRA." *The Reference Shelf: Guns in America*. Ed. Betsy Maury. Ipswich: H.W. Wilson, 2017. 66-78. Print.

APA: Draper, R. (2016). Inside the Power of the NRA. In Betsy Maury (Ed.), *The reference shelf: Guns in America* (pp. 66-78). Ipswich, MA: H.W. Wilson. (Original work published 2013)

A Criminologist's Case Against Gun Control

By Jacob Davidson
Time magazine, **December 1, 2015**

In the wake of the recent mass shooting at a Colorado Planned Parenthood that claimed three lives, President Barack Obama called the incidents of gun violence in America "not normal." "Enough is enough," Obama said. According to one count, there have been 351 mass shootings in the United States in 2015. The frequency of these shootings has led many to call for new approaches to guns and violence in America. In a Nov. 5 national survey, for instance, 52 percent of respondents said they support "stricter gun laws." (The number who said they supported "gun control" was smaller.)

In an interview, James Jacobs, director of Center for Research in Crime and Justice at New York University School of Law, a professor of constitutional law, and the author of Can Gun Control Work?, discusses what he sees as the challenges facing those who would like to change the country's approach to gun violence and gun laws.

What's the most common misunderstanding about gun control?

There are so many misunderstandings that it's hard to know where to begin. For one, we need to remember that we've have had a remarkable decrease in violent crime and gun crime in the U.S. since the early 1990s, even though the number of firearms has increased by about 10 million every year. There's no simple correspondence between the number of firearms in private hands and the amount of gun crime, and I often find it somewhat strange that there seems to be a perception that things are worse than ever when, in reality, things are really better than they've been for decades.

People should also be aware that most gun-related deaths are suicides, not murders. There are twice as many suicides in the U.S. by guns as there are homicides and I think most people find that very surprising. Over and over again one reads that 30,000 people have been killed with guns, but what's not said is that 20,000 of them took their own lives.

But perhaps the most common misperception of all, and the point I want to underline time and again is that there is no simple, effective policy to reduce gun crime that is just there for the asking as long as we have the political will to do it.

That solution doesn't exist. It's very hard to find an initiative that is implementable and enforceable that would make any kind of an impact on gun crime.

Would an assault weapon ban help prevent mass shootings?

Many people want to ban so-called assault weapons because they believe these fire-arms are uniquely dangerous, or the same as machine guns. They are not. Assault weapons—at least the ones available to civilians—are like all semi-automatics and fire one bullet with one pull of the trigger. What makes an assault weapon differ-ent than a regular rifle are the cosmetic "military-like" features, such as a bayonet mount or pistol grip and so forth, none of which have functional significance. As-sault weapons are not more powerful, they do not shoot more bullets, and they do not shoot faster. We would not be a safer society if we could eliminate all of the as-sault weapons because people could substitute for them non-assault weapons that are exactly the same.

President Obama has held up Australia and England as examples of gun control reduc-ing gun violence. Would their policies work in the U.S.?

The U.K. has gone the farthest in restricting the private ownership of guns. Shot-guns and rifles are only permitted to those who can pass through an arduous police-administered licensing process, and after the 1996 massacre in Dunblane, Scot-land, ownership of handguns was prohibited. But the U.K.'s policy could not work in the U.S. because we have a Constitution, we have a Second Amendment, and we have a Supreme Court decision that guarantees the right of Americans to keep and bear arms in their home for lawful purposes. So we cannot have a prohibition of private ownership of firearms.

Australia had a gun buyback program and prohibited new purchases of many types of firearms. We have tried gun buybacks in the United States and they have been unsuc-cessful. People do not wish to sell their guns to the government, and those who do almost invariably sell old guns so they can get the money and buy new guns. Another popular proposed policy is mandating background checks for private sales. Would that be an effective way to reduce gun crime?

I think that requiring background checks for all gun sales, period, would be a good idea in principle. The problem is implementing and enforcing such a system. There's no universal registry of firearms, so if the police were to arrest somebody and try to prosecute whoever sold them their gun without the required check, there's no way to verify who the seller was or when the sale took place. To have an effective system of regulating private sales you would need a registry, and the idea of a registry is an anathema to the gun owning community because they see a registration system as a precursor to a general confiscation—which it was in the U.K. and has been in other countries as well.

But even if we could politically will a gun registry into existence, it's unlikely that it would work. In the few states where we have a requirement that assault weapons be registered, no more than 10% of the owners of assault weapons have generally gone through the registration process, meaning at least 90% of the people don't register. Other countries have also had a difficult time making registration work. The Canadians have registered handguns since the 1930s. In 1993, the liberal government initiated shotgun and long gun registration. The program attracted a great deal of criticism, huge cost overruns and resistance from firearms owners, and in

> **The point I want to underline time and again is that there is no simple, effective policy to reduce gun crime that is just there for the asking as long as we have the political will to do it. That solution doesn't exist.**

2012 the Conservative government scrapped the program and destroyed the registry. That might give people pause for thought about the feasibility of a registration program.

Another problem with background checks is surveys of inmates show overwhelmingly that criminals obtain guns on the black market or the grey market. Almost no prison inmates say they went to a licensed dealer and filled out forms. And why would they? Even the lowest estimates show 30% of U.S. households own at least one firearm, making it very easy for someone banned from purchasing a gun to obtain one from a friend, family member, or fellow criminal who already has one.

Politicians on both sides of the gun control debate have supported doing more to keep guns away from the mentally ill. Would that work?

It seems sensible to practically everybody that people who are extremely mentally ill are not reliable enough to be gun owners, but building a policy around that is more complicated than one might think. The federal law says that a person who has ever been involuntarily committed to a mental hospital or who has been found by a court to be mentally defective is prevented from buying a firearm, but that would disqualify a very small number of people.

If we wanted to move beyond this, we'd have to expand the definition of who is mentally ill—no easy task—and even if we did, the government has had a difficult time getting mental illness data on individuals because many in the mental health treatment community strongly oppose these types of controls. They believe mental disqualifications are stigmatizing, that they would deter people from seeking treatment, and that they are detrimental to the therapeutic relationship. As a result, there's been strong opposition from these groups when more aggressive laws on guns and mental illness are proposed.

In your view what's the most effective thing the U.S. can do to reduce gun violence?

I think we need to work on law enforcement strategies aiming at the people who are most likely to commit gun crimes, so we're looking at drug dealers, gang members, people who have engaged in violent crime in the past, and the areas in which they operate. We should also draw a line in the sand—a serious red line—that if you commit a gun crime, you're going to do a lot of prison time. That policy is uncontroversial and we can work off that consensus.

Of course, even that approach won't catch everybody—there is just no overall panacea to the problem of gun violence—but I think we should be talking in terms of crime control rather than trying keep irresponsible and dangerous people from getting a weapon in the first place.

Print Citations

CMS: Davidson, Jacob. "A Criminologist's Case Against Gun Control." In *The Reference Shelf: Guns in America*, edited by Betsy Maury, 79-82. Ipswich, MA: H.W. Wilson, 2017.

MLA: Davidson, Jacob. "A Criminologist's Case Against Gun Control." *The Reference Shelf: Guns in America*. Ed. Betsy Maury. Ipswich: H.W. Wilson, 2017. 79-82. Print.

APA: Davidson, J. (2016). A Criminologist's Case Against Gun Control. In Betsy Maury (Ed.), *The reference shelf: Guns in America* (pp. 79-82). Ipswich, MA: H.W. Wilson. (Original work published 2015)

3
A Global Perspective on Guns

President Barack Obama—surrounded by a group of people who were victims of shootings or lost loved ones to gun violence—wipes away a tear during remarks announcing executive orders on background checks for gun purchases in Washington, D.C. on Tuesday, Jan. 5, 2016.

Guns in the Global Sphere

The United States is a unique nation. As the world's economic leader and one of the most culturally innovative nations on the planet, the United States has had tremendous international impact and the idea that the United States is fundamentally "better" than other nations is a deeply cherished belief for many Americans. For some Americans, patriotism and nationalistic ideology foster a deeply critical attitude about foreign nations and governments, in a similar way to how fans of certain sports teams express critical and prejudicial attitudes towards rival teams and their fans. Americans, like residents of any other nations, are free to believe that their nation is superior, but such attitudes are emotional rather than rational, largely prejudicial, and ultimately stultifying. Whether or not some Americans are comfortable with the idea, the United States is, and has always been, part of a global community and, given the increasingly intimate economic connections between all nations, the United States will increasingly be working with other countries, rather than independently, to solve essential global issues. Gun control and gun rights are global issues and nations around the world have struggled to balance public safety and personal freedom in creating policies on guns. Examining how foreign efforts to address the issue have succeeded and/or failed can provide useful information for those in the United States, on either side of the debate, who believe gun policy is in need of reform.

Gun Ownership

The Small Arms Survey is an independent research organization in Switzerland that seeks to provide data on firearms violence to governments and organizations debating gun policies. The Small Arms Survey conducted a survey of civilian firearm ownership in 2007 in which the United States came in first in gun ownership out of 30 developed nations for which data was available, with 88.8 guns per 100 people. The nation with the next highest number of guns, per capita, was Yemen, which had 54.8 per 100, followed by Switzerland, which had 45.7 per 100 people.[1] Since 2007, the number of civilian-owned guns in the United States has increased in comparison to the increase in the population. Data from the Bureau of Alcohol, Tobacco, Firearms, and Explosives, updated as of 2013, suggests that the US now has over 357 million legal guns (and a population of 321 million), which means that there are more guns than people.[2] By a wide margin, the United States is an outlier in gun ownership. Constituting roughly 5 percent of the global population, estimates indicate that the United States owns 35 to 50 percent of all legal firearms in the world.[3,4]

Gun Violence around the World

While not necessarily connected to higher levels of legal gun ownership, the United States also has higher levels of gun violence than any other developed nation. A 2013 international study on violent gun deaths found that the United States had 3.55 per 100,000 people, which was far higher than any other nation in Western Europe, with the next highest being Portugal, with 0.66 per 100,000. Compared to 21 nations in Central and Eastern Europe, in which most countries measured are considered "developing" nations, the United States ranked second, with Albania having a higher rate with 5.86 per 100,000, many of which are due to "blood feuds" in rural Albania, a unique problem without a corollary in the United States. The United States ranks second, (behind Iraq) when compared to 21 nations in North Africa and the Middle East, eighth out of 43 nations comprising Sub-Saharan Africa, and third out of 19 nations in East Asia and Southeast Asia. The most favorable comparison was in the Americas, where the United States ranked thirteenth out of 20 nations for which statistics were compiled and had far, far lower rates of gun violence than nations like El Salvador, which recorded 52.39 violent gun deaths per 100,000 people. Taken as a whole, reviews of crime data indicate that the United States has lower levels of gun violence than nations where armed gangs and governmental turbulence creates more violent gun cultures, but significantly higher levels of gun violence than any other developed, economically stable nation.[5]

While some might feel it is common sense to assume that America's extremely high numbers of civilian guns is connected to the nation's unfortunately high levels of gun violence, such an assumption cannot be independently proven and it is therefore irresponsible to suggest that the two phenomena are causally linked. There are numerous factors influencing crime rates and high crime rates are, in part, a major motivation for civilian gun ownership, whether or not owning weapons legitimately makes civilians safer. In 2014, the Federal Bureau of Investigation (FBI) calculated 1,165,383 violent crimes nationwide (a decrease of 0.2 percent from the previous year and 6.9 percent from 2010). Approximately 1.2 percent of these crimes were homicides and guns were used in 67.9 percent of murders. These statistics, while not constituting a connection between gun ownership and gun violence, do indicate that firearms are, by a significant margin, the most common tool for murder in the United States.[6] According to the Global Peace Index, the United States is the sixty-first most dangerous out of 163 nations in the world, being slightly less dangerous than living in Cambodia and slightly more dangerous than living in Guinea, Uganda, or the Dominican Republic. The 2016 report lists Syria as the most dangerous nation in the world, followed by the South Sudan, Iraq, Afghanistan, Somalia, and Yemen.[7]

Case Studies in Strict Gun Control

The United Kingdom has never had a problem with gun violence approaching the levels seen in the United States, though some United Kingdom cities do have significant levels of crime. From the 1990s to 2017, the most common method of murder in the United Kingdom was by a sharp instrument rather than a firearm. However, after the 1996 Dunblane Massacre, a mass shooting in which Thomas Hamilton, who had been accused of pedophilia, killed sixteen five- to six-year-old students and their teacher at Dunblane Primary School. The public demanded gun control and the UK enacted a ban on handguns and imposed penalties for illegal gun owner-ship that included fines and up to ten years in prison. In the United Kingdom, gun ownership is not a right, but is a "privildge" and this difference in governmental ap-proach streamlined the process of enacting more severe restrictions.[8]

Pro-gun groups in the United States have enthusiastically attacked UK policy as proof that strict gun bans do not work. In the years following the 1996 ban, the rate of gun crimes rose, peaking at 24,094 in 2003. However, since 2003, gun crimes have fallen each year. The 2015 report by the UK's Office for National Statistics reported the nation's lowest recorded crime rates since 1981, though 2016 saw an increase in crime, which police and criminologists have attributed to tensions over increased immigration.[9] As of 2017, there is little evidence to suggest that the gun ban either reduced or increased the crime rate and the UK experience, therefore, does not provide strong support for the effectiveness of strict firearms bans. How-ever, a majority of UK residents support their tough gun laws and feel safer because of them. A 2005 Gallup Poll, for instance, found that only 5 percent of Britons fa-vored liberalizing gun laws, while 79 percent wanted *more* restrictive laws than were already in place.[10] Whether or not the UK's gun laws have prevented crimes, the UK experience is a refutation of the idea that when legal gun ownership is curtailed, there is more gun crime and more potential for terrorism.

Australia also enacted strict gun-control legislation after a mass shooting, the 1996 Port Arthur Massacre in which Tasmanian resident Martin Bryant used two legally-purchased semiautomatic rifles to kill 35 in Port Arthur. In response, Austra-lia launched a series of new gun-control laws, including an almost total prohibition on automatic and semiautomatic assault weapons, in an effort to eliminate mass shootings. Australia enacted additional gun-control measures after another high-profile shooting in 2002 in Melbourne.[11]

The effectiveness of Australia's gun control policies is, like the United Kingdom, subject to debate. A June 2016 study published in the *Journal of the American Medi-cal Association* found that, while the rate of firearms deaths (including both suicides and homicides) was declining by 3 percent per year before the 1996 legislation, the rate has since fallen by 5 percent per year. Further, in the 18 years before the ban, Australia had 13 mass shootings, defined as shootings in which 5 or more people were killed, whereas there have been no mass shootings in the 20 years since the ban.[12] Furthermore, researchers found that the reduction in firearms deaths and homicides was strongest for deaths involving the specific types of weapons banned in the 1997 law.

It is difficult to use the experience of the United Kingdom or Australia to predict the result of more stringent gun regulations in the United States, which maintains an aggressively pro-gun culture unequaled in any other Western nation. In addi-tion, because Britain and Australia are islands, it is substantially easier for their governments to control the influx of illegal weapons. For the US gun lobby, the laws enacted in both the United Kingdom and Australia represent a worst-case scenario and proponents of gun rights have therefore repeatedly attacked the UK legislation as ineffective in reducing gun crime. This perception is partly accurate, though academics in the United Kingdom generally believe that the legislation has led to a slow, incremental reduction in gun crime. In Australia, the program has been successful and, despite fake news articles circulated in the United States in the early 2000s claiming that Australia had seen a dramatic increase in crime since enacting their legislation, there have been no legitimate studies refuting the effectiveness of Australia's efforts to reduce gun violence. Both cases can also be interpreted as providing significant evidence against the assertion that gun control emboldens criminals and leads to higher crime rates. Claims to the contrary are not based on legitimate data and have been created and promoted to motivate the American public against supporting similar legislation in the United States.

Micah L. Issitt

Works Used

"2016 Global Peace Index." *Vision of Humanity*. Institute for Economics and Peace. IEP Report 39. June 2016. Pdf. 28 Dec 2016.

Brennan, Allison. "Analysis: Fewer US Gun Owners Own More Guns." *CNN Politics*. Jul 31 2012. Web. 28 Dec 2016.

Chapman, Simon, Alpers, Philip, and Michael Jones. "Association Between Gun Law Reforms and Intentional Firearm Deaths in Australia, 1979-2013." *Journal of the American Medical Association*, Vol. 316, No. 3, July 19, 2016, 291–99.

"Crime in the United States 2014." *FBI*. Federal Bureau of Investigation. Criminal Justice Information Services Division. 2014. Pdf. 28 Dec 2016.

Flatley, John. "Crime in England and Wales: Year Ending March 2015." ONS. Office for National Statistics. Jul 16 2015. Web. 28 Dec 2016.

Ingraham, Christopher. "There Are Now More Guns Than People in the United States." *The Washington Post*. Oct 5 2015. Web. 27 Dec 2016.

Karp, Aaron. "Small Arms Survey 2007." *Small Arms Survey*. 2007. Pdf. 27 Dec 2016.

Kelto, Anders. "The US Is a World Leader in Gun Deaths." *NPR*. National Public Radio. Dec 7 2015. Web. 27 Dec 2016.

Krause, William J. "Gun Control Legislation." *Congressional Research Service*. Federation of American Scientists. Nov 14 2016. Web. 28 Dec 2016.

Masters, Jonathan. "Gun Control around the World: A Primer." *The Atlantic*. Atlantic Monthly Group. Jan 12 2016. Web. 28 Dec 2016.

Mika, Shelley. "Britons Aim for Tougher Gun Laws." *Gallup*. Gallup Inc. Jun 21 2005. Web. 28 Dec 2016.

Wilkinson, Peter. "Dunblane: How UK School Massacre Led to Tighter Gun Control." *CNN*. Cable News Network. Jan 30 2013. Web. 28 Dec 2016.

Notes

1. Karp, "Small Arms Survey 2007."
2. Ingraham, "There Are Now More Guns Than People in the United States."
3. Brennan, "Analysis: Fewer US Gun Owners Own More Guns."
4. Krause, "Gun Control Legislation."
5. Kelto, "The US Is a World Leader in Gun Deaths."
6. "Crime in the United States 2014," *Federal Bureau of Investigation*.
7. "2016 Global Peace Index," *Vision of Humanity*.
8. Wilkinson, "Dunblane: How UK School Massacre Led to Tighter Gun Control."
9. Flatley, "Crime in England and Wales: Year Ending March 2015."
10. Mika, "Britons Aim for Tougher Gun Laws."
11. Masters, "Gun Control Around the World: A Primer."
12. Chapman, Alpers, and Jones, "Association Between Gun Law Reforms and Intentional Firearm Deaths in Australia, 1979–2013."

Why America Isn't the Only Country That Wants Guns for Self-Defense

By Jennifer Carlson

The Christian Science Monitor, March 11, 2013

Tony Martin, a British farm owner, shot and killed Fred Barras, a home intruder, in 1999. Neighborhood Watch volunteer George Zimmerman, of Sanford, Fla., shot to death 17-year-old Trayvon Martin a year ago. And last month, South Africa's "Blade Runner," Oscar Pistorius, shot and killed his model girlfriend Reeva Steenkamp, whom he claims to have mistaken for a home intruder. All three faced—or currently face—criminal charges in connection with the shootings. All have claimed self-defense.

These sensationalized cases from across the globe suggest that the American penchant for firearms is less exceptional than many in the United States may think. The appeal of guns is global. Civilians in Mexico have started "self-policing" in the wake of increased fears of crime and inadequate public law enforcement. In India, after the New Delhi gang rape in December 2012, women's demands for gun permits have escalated precipitously. Even Britain is seeing small but meaningful increases in gun permits amid concerns about increasing crime and police efficacy, according to *The Guardian* newspaper.

If Americans want to move forward in our national conversation about gun control, we need to understand gun culture less as an example of American pathology or a source of US pride (depending on what side of the debate you take), and more as a social practice embedded in inequality, violence, and fear that are aggravated in the US, but not unique to it.

Americans like to think of themselves and their society as unique. In our national gun debate, this means emphasizing the Second Amendment, a hunting heritage, and the general ethos of rugged individualism that set Americans apart. For gun-rights advocates, these are virtues to celebrate; for gun control advocates, these are often seen more as roadblocks in the path toward sensible gun control already adopted by our European counterparts.

There is no doubt that America's gun ownership stands out globally: With an estimated 300 million-plus guns in the hands of civilians, Americans own more guns than any other nation in the world. And without America's particular legal foundations and history, it is hard to imagine that the country would be as much of a hotbed for gun rights as it is today.

> The appeal of guns for personal protection is hardly unique to America. Consider gun ownership in South Africa, Britain, India, and Mexico. All these societies are dealing with inequality exacerbated by economic austerity and eroding public services, which breeds fear about insecurity.

But the appeal of guns for self-defense and personal protection purposes is hardly a simple case of American exceptionalism. Consider South Africa, Britain, India, and beyond.

India does not have a constitutional equivalent of the Second Amendment, but amid fears of crime, gun proponents are organizing in groups like the National Association for Gun Rights in India. And South Africa's "private defence" law allows citizens to defend themselves and others not unlike America's controversial "stand your ground" laws. Like Mr. Pistorius, millions of South Africans sleep next to a firearm.

Guns in America, India, South Africa, Britain, Mexico: What do these societies have in common?

All are dealing with the unfinished business of racial and gender inequality that have been exacerbated by economic austerity measures, a renewed focus on crime and criminal justice, and public services in crisis. These are societies that breed rampant fears and concerns about insecurity (if at times disproportionate to the actual rates of crime) and the sense that the police cannot, or will not, provide protection to the average citizen.

As one armed, Indian woman said to a reporter for The Guardian, "I don't have faith in the police to protect me. There are so many attacks on women these days. It's everybody's right to defend themselves. I think all women who are vulnerable should be carrying guns."

Guns may be as "American as apple pie," but they are not exclusively American because the problems that drive people to guns are not exclusive to the US.

Taking a global look at guns reveals the folly in gun debates that focus merely on regulating and restricting guns themselves. To address guns, we must also address why people—in America and elsewhere—are turning to them in the first place.

Print Citations

CMS: Carlson, Jennifer. "Why America Isn't the Only Country That Wants Guns for Self-Defense." In *The Reference Shelf: Guns in America*, edited by Betsy Maury, 91-92. Ipswich, MA: H.W. Wilson, 2017.

MLA: Carlson, Jennifer. "Why America Isn't the Only Country That Wants Guns for Self-Defense." *The Reference Shelf: Guns in America*. Ed. Betsy Maury. Ipswich: H.W. Wilson, 2017. 91-92. Print.

APA: Carlson, J. (2016). Why America isn't the only country that wants guns for self-defense. In Betsy Maury (Ed.), *The reference shelf: Guns in America* (pp. 91-92). Ipswich, MA: H.W. Wilson. (Original work published 2013)

Why the Gun Lobby Is Winning

The Economist, **April 4, 2015**

When a young man walked into an elementary school in Newtown, Connecticut in December 2012 and murdered 20 small children and six staff with a Bushmaster rifle from his mother's gun collection, some wondered if a tipping-point had been reached. Surely America would now enact laws to keep lethal weapons out of the wrong hands?

No chance. Bids to curb sales of the most powerful guns and largest-capacity magazines failed. Congress even refused to expand the number of gun-buyers checked for histories of crime or severe mental illness—though 90% of Americans support such checks. In March this year federal regulators dropped a bid to ban a type of bullet that can pierce body armour, of the sort that police often wear, after 285 Republican and seven Democratic members of Congress objected.

The gun lobby's winning record has done little to make its members less angry. The National Rifle Association (NRA), a deep-pocketed group with 5m members, accuses Barack Obama's administration of a "relentless assault" on the constitutional right of citizens to keep and bear arms. Actual evidence of federal tyranny is a bit meagre—in part because the NRA is so good at whipping Washington politicians into line. No matter. A current "trending" alert from the NRA's Institute for Legislative Action sounds the alarm about a rule tweak for hunters taking guns on overseas trips, who—rather than filling out a form at home—may now have to wait at the airport while a customs officer enters their details into a computer. This, the NRA asserts, raises alarming questions about hunters' information being stored by the feds, and is part of a "pattern of abuse" suggesting that Mr Obama's final years in office may be the "most challenging" in the history of American gun-ownership.

To prevent gun deaths, politicians offer— more guns

Meanwhile children keep getting shot at school, sometimes by other children. In the first two years after Newtown there were at least 95 shootings at American schools and colleges, resulting in 45 deaths, according to a tally by Everytown for Gun Safety, a gun-control campaign. After Newtown a few states moved to curb sales of the deadliest weapons. Since 2012 five states have expanded background checks on gun buyers, closing loopholes left by Congress (a bill proposed on March 26th would make Oregon the sixth). But many more states have relaxed firearms laws.

Gun-advocates do not win all their fights in the states, but 2015 still looks like a banner year for them. Republicans enjoyed sweeping wins at the state level in elections last November, allowing the party's representatives to advance cherished goals during the short, intense legislative sessions under way in state capitals. In lots of places, those goals involve more guns.

Often, gun-lovers hew to a familiar conservative line: that crime is deterred when upstanding citizens pack heat. Florida is debating a "school safety" bill allowing superintendents to choose staff or volunteers with police or military backgrounds to serve as armed school guards. Iowa is pondering a law that would let children younger than 14 use pistols and revolvers (with adult supervision, legislators hasten to add). Republicans in Arkansas want to allow armed judges in courtrooms. Bills were proposed this year in 16 states to overturn gun bans on college campuses, and remain under debate in a dozen states.

Some argue that arming female students will deter rapists. As Michele Fiore, a Republican assemblywoman in Nevada, said to the *New York Times*: "If these young, hot little girls on campus have a firearm, I wonder how many men will want to assault them?" Others retort that arming potential rapists might be less helpful. William McRaven, the new chancellor of the University of Texas System, declared that concealed handguns

> The gun lobby's winning record has done little to make its members less angry. The National Rifle Association (NRA), a deep-pocketed group with 5m members, accuses Barack Obama's administration of a "relentless assault" on the constitutional right of citizens to keep and bear arms.

would make his 210,000 students less safe. As a former navy Seal, Admiral McRaven is hard to portray as a hand-wringing squish, and "campus carry" may well not pass the Texas legislature. To soothe activists for whom gun rights are a test of conservative purity, Republican leaders seem likely to embrace the once-arcane issue of "open carry", allowing the roughly 825,000 Texans with concealed-handgun licences to carry pistols and revolvers visibly (Texans already carry rifles without restriction).

Some would like to go much further. The fieriest arguments of 2015 involve "constitutional carry"—the claim that the constitution's second amendment is the only permit Americans need, allowing citizens to carry a concealed or visible gun without any licence, checks or training. Such laws already exist in Alaska, Arizona, Arkansas, Vermont and Wyoming. Legislators in Kansas just approved a version. So did lawmakers in West Virginia and Montana. The governor of West Virginia, a Democrat in his final term, vetoed a bill (though, like several rural states, West Virginia allows open carry without a permit). Montana's governor, a Democrat, vetoed a bill too, though his state allows permit-less guns outside cities. Maine is weighing a constitutional carry bill.

Lethal Force for All

The NRA can never declare victory, for then what would be the point of it? After each concession, it demands more. Some day, perhaps, it will ask for something so outrageous that it sparks a backlash. But for now it strikes a chord. For the first time in two decades a new poll by the Pew Research Centre found more Americans supporting gun rights than gun controls. How can this be so, when such a huge majority favour background checks? The answer is that background checks are tools of the state and trust in the state has plunged in the past decade, notably on the right where it blends with loathing for Mr Obama. Wayne LaPierre, the NRA's charismatic frontman, told a conservative crowd in February that when criminals attack, or wives, sisters and daughters face assault through "a kicked-down door", "laws can't protect you…You're on your own." That is the authentic voice of the gun lobby in 2015. Fear smothers rational debate. It is meant to.

Print Citations

CMS: "Why the Gun Lobby Is Winning." In *The Reference Shelf: Guns in America*, edited by Betsy Maury, 94-96. Ipswich, MA: H.W. Wilson, 2017.

MLA: "Why the Gun Lobby Is Winning." *The Reference Shelf: Guns in America*. Ed. Betsy Maury. Ipswich: H.W. Wilson, 2017. 94-96. Print.

APA: The Economist. (2017). Why the gun lobby is winning. In Betsy Maury (Ed.), *The reference shelf: Guns in America* (pp. 94-96). Ipswich, MA: H.W. Wilson. (Original work published 2015)

US Gun Policy: Global Comparisons

By Jonathan Masters

Council on Foreign Relations, January 12, 2016

Introduction

The debate over gun control in the United States has waxed and waned over the years, stirred by a series of mass killings by gunmen in civilian settings. In particular, the killing of twenty schoolchildren in Newtown, Connecticut, in December 2012 fueled a national discussion over gun laws and calls by the Obama administration to limit the availability of military-style weapons. However, compromise legislation that would have banned semiautomatic assault weapons and expanded background checks was defeated in the Senate in 2013, despite extensive public support.

Gun control advocates sought to rekindle the debate following another string of deadly mass shootings in 2015, including the killing of nine people at a church in Charleston, South Carolina, and fourteen at a community center in San Bernardino, California. These advocates often highlight the stricter gun laws and lower incidents of gun violence in several other democracies, like Japan and Australia, but many others say this correlation proves little and note that rates of gun crime in the United States have plunged over the last two decades.

In January 2016, President Obama took a series of executive actions intended to curb gun violence, including measures to expand federal background checks to most gun buyers.

United States

The Second Amendment of the US Constitution states: "A well-regulated Militia, being necessary to the security of a free State, the right of the people to keep and bear Arms, shall not be infringed." Supreme Court rulings, citing this amendment, have upheld the right of states to regulate firearms. However, in a 2008 decision (*District of Columbia v. Heller*) confirming an individual right to keep and bear arms, the court struck down Washington, DC, laws that banned handguns and required those in the home to be locked or disassembled.

A number of gun advocates consider ownership a birthright and an essential part of the nation's heritage. The United States, with less than 5 percent of the world's population, has about 35–50 percent of the world's civilian-owned guns, according to a 2007 report by the Switzerland-based Small Arms Survey. It ranks number one in firearms per capita. The United States also has the highest homicide-by-firearm rate among the world's most developed nations.

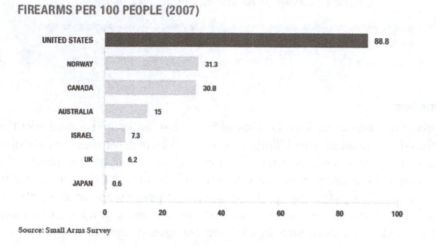

FIREARMS PER 100 PEOPLE (2007)

Source: Small Arms Survey

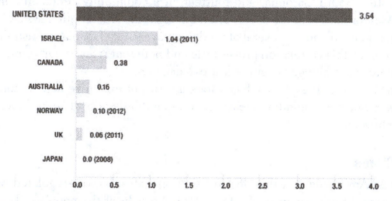

FIREARM HOMICIDES PER 100,000 PEOPLE (2013)

Sources: gunpolicy.org, University of Sydney

Credits: Jonathan Masters, Julia Ro

COUNCIL on
FOREIGN
RELATIONS

But many gun rights proponents say these statistics do not indicate a cause-and-effect relationship and note that the rates of gun homicide and other gun crimes in the United States have dropped since highs in the early 1990s.

Federal law sets the minimum standards for firearm regulation in the United States, but individual states have their own laws, some of which provide further restrictions, others which are more lenient. Some states, including Idaho, Alaska, and Kansas, have passed laws designed to circumvent federal policies, but the Constitution (Article VI, Paragraph 2) establishes the supremacy of federal law.

The Gun Control Act of 1968 prohibited the sale of firearms to several categories of individuals, including persons under eighteen years of age, those with criminal records, the mentally disabled, unlawful aliens, dishonorably discharged military personnel, and others. In 1993, the law was amended by the Brady Handgun Violence Prevention Act, which mandated background checks for all unlicensed persons purchasing a firearm from a federally licensed dealer.

In January 2016, President Obama issued a package of executive actions designed to decrease gun violence, notably a measure to require dealers selling firearms at gun shows or online to obtain federal licenses and, in turn, conduct background checks of prospective buyers. Gun control advocates hope these steps will help close existing legal loopholes that have allowed violent criminals and others to purchase weapons without FBI screening.

Additionally, he proposed new funding to hire hundreds more federal law enforcement agents, and budgeting $500 million to expand access to mental health care. (Suicides, many by individuals with undiagnosed mental illness, account for about 60 percent of gun deaths.) The president said he was compelled to move on this issue under his own authority because Congress had failed to pass "common-sense gun safety reforms."

As of 2016, there were no federal laws banning semiautomatic assault weapons, military-style .50 caliber rifles, handguns, or large-capacity ammunition magazines, which can increase the potential lethality of a given firearm. There was a federal prohibition on assault weapons and high-capacity magazines between 1994 and 2004, but Congress allowed these restrictions to expire.

The United States, with less than 5 percent of the world's population, has about 35–50 percent of the world's civilian-owned guns, according to a 2007 report by the Switzerland-based Small Arms Survey.

Canada

Many analysts characterize Canada's gun laws as strict in comparison to the United States, while others say recent developments have eroded safeguards. Ottawa, like Washington, sets federal gun restrictions that the provinces, territories, and municipalities can supplement. Federal regulations require all gun owners, who must be at least eighteen years of age, to obtain a license that includes a background check and a public safety course.

There are three classes of weapons: nonrestricted (e.g., ordinary rifles and shotguns), restricted (e.g., handguns, semiautomatic rifles/shotguns, and sawed-offs), and prohibited (e.g., automatics). A person wishing to acquire a restricted firearm must obtain a federal registration certificate, according to the Royal Canadian Mounted Police.

Modern Canadian gun laws have been driven by prior gun violence. In December 1989, a disgruntled student walked into a Montreal engineering school with a semiautomatic rifle and killed fourteen students and injured over a dozen others. The incident is widely credited with driving subsequent gun legislation, including the 1995 Firearms Act, which required owner licensing and the registration of all long guns (i.e., rifles and shotguns) while banning more than half of all registered guns. However, in 2012, the government abandoned the long-gun registry, citing cost concerns.

Australia

The inflection point for modern gun control in Australia was the Port Arthur massacre of April 1996, when a young man killed thirty-five people and wounded twenty-three others. The rampage, perpetrated with a semiautomatic rifle, was the worst mass shooting in the nation's history. Less than two weeks later, the conservative-led national government pushed through fundamental changes to the country's gun laws in cooperation with the various states, which regulate firearms.

The National Agreement on Firearms all but prohibited automatic and semiautomatic assault rifles, stiffened licensing and ownership rules, and instituted a temporary gun buyback program that took some 650,000 assault weapons (about one-sixth of the national stock) out of public circulation. Among other things, the law also required licensees to demonstrate a "genuine need" for a particular type of gun and take a firearm safety course. After another high-profile shooting in Melbourne in 2002, Australia's handgun laws were tightened as well.

Many analysts say these measures have been highly effective, citing declining gun-death rates, and the fact that there have been no gun-related mass killings in Australia since 1996. Many also suggest the policy response in the wake of Port Arthur could serve as a model for the United States.

Israel

Military service is compulsory in Israel and guns are very much a part of everyday life. By law, most eighteen-year-olds are drafted, psychologically screened, and receive at least some weapons training after high school. After serving typically two or three years in the armed forces, however, most Israelis are discharged and must abide by civilian gun laws.

The country has relatively strict gun regulations, including an assault-weapons ban and a requirement to register ownership with the government. To become licensed, an applicant must be an Israeli citizen or a permanent resident, be at least twenty-one-years-old, and speak at least some Hebrew, among other qualifications. Notably, a person must also show genuine cause to carry a firearm, such as self-defense or hunting.

However, some critics question the efficacy of these measures. "It doesn't take much of an expert to realize that these restrictions, in and of themselves, do not constitute much by the way of gun control," writes Liel Leibovitz for the Jewish magazine *Tablet*. He notes the relative ease with which someone can justify owning a gun, including residing in an Israeli settlement, employment as a security guard, or working with valuables or large sums of money. Furthermore, he explains that almost the entire population has indirect access to an assault weapon by either being a soldier or a reservist or a relative of one. Israel's relatively low gun-related homicide rate is a product of the country's unique "gun culture," he says.

United Kingdom

Modern gun control efforts in the United Kingdom have been precipitated by extraordinary acts of violence that sparked public outrage and, eventually, political action. In August 1987, a lone gunman armed with two legally owned semi-automatic rifles and a handgun went on a six-hour shooting spree roughly seventy miles west of London, killing sixteen people and then himself. In the wake of the incident, known as the Hungerford massacre, Britain introduced the Firearms (Amendment) Act, which expanded the list of banned weapons, including certain semiautomatic rifles, and increased registration requirements for other weapons.

> A number of gun advocates consider ownership a birthright and an essential part of the nation's heritage. The United States, with less than 5 percent of the world's population, has about 35–50 percent of the world's civilian-owned guns, according to a 2007 report by the Switzerland-based Small Arms Survey.

A gun-related tragedy in the Scottish town of Dunblane, in 1996, prompted Britain's strictest gun laws yet. In March of that year, a middle-aged man armed with four legally purchased handguns shot and killed sixteen young schoolchildren and one adult before committing suicide in the country's worst mass shooting to date. The incident sparked a public campaign known as the Snowdrop Petition, which helped drive legislation banning handguns, with few exceptions. The government also instituted a temporary gun buyback program, which many credit with taking tens of thousands of illegal or unwanted guns out of supply.

However, the effectiveness of Britain's gun laws in gun-crime reduction over the last twenty-five years has stirred ongoing debate. Analysts note that the number of such crimes grew heavily in the late 1990s and peaked in 2004 before falling with each subsequent year. "While tighter gun control removes risk on an incremental basis," said Peter Squires, a Brighton University criminologist, in an interview with CNN, "significant numbers of weapons remain in Britain."

Norway

Gun control had rarely been much of a political issue in Norway—where gun laws are viewed as tough, but ownership rates are high—until right-wing extremist Anders Behring Breivik killed seventy-seven people in an attack on an island summer camp in July 2011. Though Norway ranked tenth worldwide in gun ownership, according to the Small Arms Survey, it placed near the bottom in gun-homicide rates. (The US rate is roughly sixty-four times higher.) Most Norwegian police, much like the British, do not carry firearms.

In the wake of the tragedy, some analysts in the United States cited Breivik's rampage as proof that strict gun laws—which in Norway include requiring applicants to be at least eighteen years of age, specify a "valid reason" for gun ownership, and obtain a government license—are ineffective. "Those who are willing to break the laws against murder do not care about the regulation of firearms, and will get a hold of weapons whether doing so is legal or not," wrote Charles C. W. Cooke in *National Review*. Other gun-control critics have argued that had other Norwegians, including the police, been armed, Breivik might have been stopped earlier and killed fewer victims. An independent commission after the massacre recommended tightening Norway's gun restrictions in a number of ways, including prohibiting pistols and semiautomatic weapons.

Japan

Gun-control advocates regularly cite Japan's highly restrictive firearm regulations in tandem with its extraordinarily low gun-homicide rate, which is the lowest in the world at one in ten million, according to the latest data available. Most guns are illegal in the country and ownership rates, which are quite small, reflect this.

Under Japan's firearm and sword law, the only guns permitted are shotguns, air guns, guns that have research or industrial purposes, or those used for competitions. However, before access to these specialty weapons is granted, one must obtain formal instruction and pass a battery of written, mental, and drug tests and a rigorous background check. Furthermore, owners must inform the authorities of how the weapon and ammunition is stored and provide the firearm for annual inspection.

Some analysts link Japan's aversion to firearms with its demilitarization in the aftermath of World War II. Others say that because the overall crime rate in the country is so low, most Japanese see no need for firearms.

Print Citations

CMS: Masters, Jonathan. "U.S. Gun Policy: Global Comparisons." In *The Reference Shelf: Guns in America*, edited by Betsy Maury, 97-102. Ipswich, MA: H.W. Wilson, 2017.

MLA: Masters, Jonathan. "U.S. Gun Policy: Global Comparisons." *The Reference Shelf: Guns in America*. Ed. Betsy Maury. Ipswich: H.W. Wilson, 2017. 97-102. Print.

APA: Masters, J. (2017). U.S. gun policy: Global comparisons. In Betsy Maury (Ed.), *The reference shelf: Guns in America* (pp. 97-102). Ipswich, MA: H.W. Wilson. (Original work published 2016)

How US Gun Control Compares to the Rest of the World

By John Donahue

The Conversation, June 24, 2015

In June the Charleston killings renewed the sporadic debates over whether gun control might have prevented this terrible tragedy. Four months on, the massacre at Umpqua Community College in Roseburg, Oregon has left nine dead.

And once again, as after Charleston, President Obama has spoken openly about his frustration with the fact that "this kind of mass violence does not happen in other advanced countries."

On October 1st he put it this way:

We know that other countries, in response to one mass shooting, have been able to craft laws that almost eliminate mass shootings. Friends of ours, allies of ours – Great Britain, Australia, countries like ours. So we know there are ways to prevent it.

So far, however, the US has not come up with "ways to prevent it." The National Rifle Association (NRA), it seems, has so much power over politicians that even when 90% of Americans (including a majority of NRA members) wanted universal background checks to be adopted following the Newtown killings of 2012, no federal action ensued. Certainly, the type of comprehensive response that has been effective in other countries is unlike to emerge in the United States.

The NRA stranglehold on appropriate anti-crime measures is only part of the problem, though.

The gun culture's worship of the magical protective capacities of guns and their power to be wielded against perceived enemies—including the federal government —is a message that resonates with troubled individuals from the Santa Barbara killer, who was seeking vengeance on women who had failed to perceive his greatness, to the Charleston killer who echoed the Tea Party mantra of taking back our country.

I've been researching gun violence—and what can be done to prevent it—in the US for 25 years. The fact is that if NRA claims about the efficacy of guns in reducing crime were true, the US would have the lowest homicide rate among industrialized nations instead of the highest homicide rate (by a wide margin).

The US is by far the world leader in the number of guns in civilian hands. The stricter gun laws of other "advanced countries" have restrained homicidal violence, suicides and gun accidents—even when, in some cases, laws were introduced over massive protests from their armed citizens.

The State of Gun Control in the US

Eighteen states in the US and a number of cities including Chicago, New York and San Francisco have tried to reduce the unlawful use of guns as well as gun accidents by adopting laws to keep guns safely stored when they are not in use. Safe storage is a common form of gun regulation in nations with stricter gun regulations.

The NRA has been battling such laws for years. But that effort was dealt a blow earlier this month when the US Supreme Court—over a strident dissent by Justices Thomas and Scalia—refused to consider the San Francisco law that required guns not in use be stored safely. This was undoubtedly a positive step because hundreds of thousands of guns are stolen every year, and good public policy must try to keep guns out of the hands of criminals and children.

The dissenters, however, were alarmed by the thought that a gun stored in a safe would not be immediately available for use, but they seemed unaware of how unusual it is that a gun is helpful when someone is under attack.

For starters, only the tiniest fraction of victims of violent crime are able to use a gun in their defense. Over the period from 2007-2011, when roughly six million nonfatal violent crimes occurred each year, data from the National Crime Victimization Survey show that the victim did not defend with a gun in 99.2% of these incidents—this in a country with 300 million guns in civilian hands.

In fact, a study of 198 cases of unwanted entry into occupied single-family dwellings in Atlanta (not limited to night when the residents were sleeping) found that the invader was twice as likely to obtain the victim's gun than to have the victim use a firearm in self-defense.

The author of the study, Arthur Kellerman, concluded in words that Justice Thomas and Scalia might well heed: On average, the gun that represents the greatest threat is the one that is kept loaded and readily available in a bedside drawer.

A loaded, unsecured gun in the home is like an insurance policy that fails to deliver at least 95% of the time you need it, but has the constant potential—particularly in the case of handguns that are more easily manipulated by children and more attractive for use in crime—to harm someone in the home or (via theft) the public at large.

More Guns Won't Stop Gun Violence

For years, the NRA mantra has been that allowing citizens to carry concealed handguns would reduce crime as they fought off or scared off the criminals.

Some early studies even purported to show that so-called right to carry laws (RTC) did just that, but a 2004 report from the National Research Council refuted that claim (saying it was not supported by "the scientific evidence"), while remaining uncertain about what the true impact of RTC laws was.

Ten years of additional data have allowed new research to get a better fix on this question, which is important since the NRA is pushing for a Supreme Court decision that would allow RTC as a matter of constitutional law.

The new research on this issue from my research team at Stanford University has given the most compelling evidence to date that RTC laws are associated with significant increases in violent crime—particularly for aggravated assault. Looking at Uniform Crime Reports data from 1979-2012, we find that, on average, the 33 states that adopted RTC laws over this period experienced violent crime rates that are 4%-19% higher after 10 years than if they had not adopted these laws.

This hardly makes a strong case for RTC as a constitutional right. At the very least more research is needed to estimate more precisely exactly how much violent crime such a decision would unleash in the states that have so far resisted the NRA-backed RTC laws.

In the meantime, can anything make American politicians listen to the preferences of the 90% on the wisdom of adopting universal background checks for gun purchases?

Gun Control Around the World

As an academic exercise, one might speculate whether law could play a constructive role in reducing the number or deadliness of mass shootings.

Most other advanced nations apparently think so, since they make it far harder for someone like the Charleston killer to get his hands on a Glock semiautomatic handgun or any other kind of firearm (universal background checks are common features of gun regulation in other developed countries).

- Germany: To buy a gun, anyone under the age of 25 has to pass a psychiatric evaluation (presumably 21-year-old Dylann Roof would have failed).

- Finland: Handgun license applicants are only allowed to purchase firearms if they can prove they are active members of regulated shooting clubs. Before they can get a gun, applicants must pass an aptitude test, submit to a police interview, and show they have a proper gun storage unit.

- Italy: To secure a gun permit, one must establish a genuine reason to possess a firearm and pass a background check considering both criminal and mental health records (again, presumably Dylann Roof would have failed).

- France: Firearms applicants must have no criminal record and pass a background check that considers the reason for the gun purchase and evaluates the criminal, mental, and health records of the applicant. (Dylann Roof would presumably have failed in this process).

- United Kingdom and Japan: Handguns are illegal for private citizens.

While mass shootings as well as gun homicides and suicides are not unknown in these countries, the overall rates are substantially higher in the United States than in these competitor nations.

While NRA supporters frequently challenge me on these statistics saying that this is only because "American blacks are so violent," it is important to note that white murder rates in the US are well over twice as high as the murder rates in any of these other countries.

Australia Hasn't Had a Mass Shooting Since 1996

The story of Australia, which had 13 mass shootings in the 18-year period from 1979 to 1996 but none in the succeeding 19 years, is worth examining.

The turning point was the 1996 Port Arthur massacre in Tasmania, in which a gunman killed 35 individuals using semiautomatic weapons.

In the wake of the massacre, the conservative federal government succeeded in implementing tough new gun control laws throughout the country. A large array of weapons were banned—including the Glock semiautomatic handgun used in the Charleston shootings. The government also imposed a mandatory gun buy back that substantially reduced gun possession in Australia.

The effect was that both gun suicides and homicides (as well as total suicides and homicides) fell. In addition, the 1996 legislation made it a crime to use firearms in self-defense.

When I mention this to disbelieving NRA supporters they insist that crime must now be rampant in Australia. In fact, the Australian murder rate has fallen to close one per 100,000 while the US rate, thankfully lower than in the early 1990s, is still roughly at 4.5 per 100,000—over four times as high. Moreover, robberies in Australia occur at only about half the rate of the US (58 in Australia versus 113.1 per 100,000 in the US in 2012).

> On average, the gun that represents the greatest threat is the one that is kept loaded and readily available in a bedside drawer.

How did Australia do it? Politically, it took a brave prime minister to face the rage of Australian gun interests.

John Howard wore a bullet-proof vest when he announced the proposed gun restrictions in June 1996. The deputy prime minister was hung in effigy. But Australia did not have a domestic gun industry to oppose the new measures so the will of the people was allowed to emerge. And today, support for the safer, gun-restricted Australia is so strong that going back would not be tolerated by the public.

That Australia hasn't had a mass shooting since 1996 is likely more than merely the result of the considerable reduction in guns—it's certainly not the case that guns have disappeared altogether.

I suspect that the country has also experienced a cultural shift between the shock of the Port Arthur massacre and the removal of guns from every day life as they are no longer available for self-defense and they are simply less present throughout the country. Troubled individuals, in other words, are not constantly being reminded that guns are a means to address their alleged grievances to the extent that they were in the past, or continue to be in the US.

Lax Gun Control in One Nation Can Create Problems in Another

Of course, strict gun regulations cannot ensure that the danger of mass shootings or killings has been eliminated.

Norway has strong gun control and committed humane values. But they didn't prevent Anders Breivik from opening fire on a youth camp on the island of Utoya in 2011? His clean criminal record and hunting license had allowed him to secure semiautomatic rifles, but Norway restricted his ability to get high-capacity clips for them. In his manifesto, Breivik wrote about his attempts to legally buy weapons, stating, "I envy our European American brothers as the gun laws in Europe sucks ass in comparison."

In fact, in the same manifesto ("December and January—Rifle/gun accessories purchased"), Breivik wrote that it was from a US supplier that he purchased—and had mailed – ten 30-round ammunition magazines for the rifle he used in his attack.

In other words, even if a particular state chooses to make it harder for some would-be killers to get their weapons, these efforts can be undercut by the jurisdictions that hold out from these efforts. In the US, of course, gun control measures at the state and local level are often thwarted by the lax attitude to gun acquisition in other states.

Print Citations

CMS: Donahue, John. "How US Gun Control Compares to the Rest of the World." In *The Reference Shelf: Guns in America*, edited by Betsy Maury, 104-08. Ipswich, MA: H.W. Wilson, 2017.

MLA: Donahue, John. "How US Gun Control Compares to the Rest of the World." *The Reference Shelf: Guns in America*. Ed. Betsy Maury. Ipswich: H.W. Wilson, 2017. 104-08. Print.

APA: Donahue, J. (2017). How US gun control compares to the rest of the world. In Betsy Maury (Ed.), *The reference shelf: Guns in America* (pp. 104-08). Ipswich, MA: H.W. Wilson. (Original work published 2015)

4
Trends in the Gun Debate

George Frey/Bloomberg via Getty Images

A sign reading 'I'll Fight for Freedom' is displayed at a gun store in Orem, Utah, U.S., on Thursday, Aug. 11, 2016. The constitutional right of Americans to bear arms was a flash point in the 2016 presidential election.

Trends in the Gun Debate

Each era brings new issues to the forefront of the gun-policy debate, often motivated by broader social issues affecting the nation. The gun debate in 2016 incorporated debates about racial violence, the increasing concern over domestic terrorism/mass shootings and the discussion about guns and mental health. The Donald Trump campaign also had an enormous effect on the gun debate during the year, as Trump's illegitimate assertions that the Democratic Party, if elected, would abolish Second Amendment freedoms, motivated a massive surge in gun purchases among those who believed that they might soon be unable to purchase a legal gun. Apparently emboldened by support from a major party candidate, the year also saw an increase in the amount of propaganda produced in support of gun rights and aimed at marketing gun sales to individuals concerned about crime, terrorism, racial tension, and alleged threats to Second Amendment rights.

Guns and Race

According to a 2013 Pew Research study, about 82 percent of gun owners are white and more than 74 percent are men, with a full 61 percent of gun owners being white men (a group that makes up 32 percent of the population).[1] A 2015 Pew Research study also found that African Americans and Hispanics/Latinos are far more likely to support gun control, with only about 24 percent in either group believing it was more important to protect the Second Amendment than to control guns.[2] Numerous statistics also indicate that gun ownership is highest where crime rates are lowest, such as in suburban and rural communities. In essence, it can be accurately stated that American gun owners are predominantly white men living in rural or suburban areas that typically have low levels of crime, population density, and racial diversity.

Researchers from Monash University in Australia took a look at statistics for gun ownership and political/cultural ideology in the United States and found that individuals who expressed "symbolic racism," defined as the tendency to believe in racial stereotypes (blacks are dangerous, blacks are lazy, etc.) are more likely to own guns.[3] An interesting trend emerges, however, when African Americans take an interest in gun rights. When militant Black Power groups began encouraging members to carry guns for self-defense in the 1960s, white Americans embraced gun control, leading to then California Governor Ronald Reagan (despite defending gun-rights during his presidency) supporting the 1967 Mulford Act, which made it illegal to carry a loaded gun in public.

The Arbitrary War on Terror

Another recent debate in gun policy concerns proposals to create legislation that would prevent terrorists from obtaining weapons. While it has been suggested that the government might use the existing "Terrorist Watch List" to prevent terrorists from purchasing legal guns, the list contains few US residents and there has been substantial controversy regarding the criteria for inclusion on the list. There is a deeper problem in preventing terrorists from obtaining guns in that the determination of what constitutes terrorism is largely subjective and influenced by racial prejudice and xenophobia. Federal law defines terrorism as violent acts "intended to intimidate or coerce a civilian population," or to influence the government or perhaps public policy. [4] So, Dylann Roof, the white supremacist who killed nine African-Americans at a South Carolina church was not designated as a terrorist, though it could be argued that his actions were intended to "intimidate or coerce" the African American population in South Carolina. [5] By contrast, there was widespread support for classifying the San Bernadino, California attack by Syed Rizwan and Tashfeen Malik as a terrorist act.

Some argue that the Rizwan and Malik crime justifies broad suspicion of all Muslims or Muslim immigrants, a viewpoint that Donald Trump promoted through proposals to create a Muslim registry in the United States. Globally and historically, however, terrorism is not an "Islamic" phenomenon. For instance, 94 percent of terrorist attacks in the United States between 1980 and 2005 were committed by non-Muslims and, in fact, more terrorist attacks were committed by Jewish extremists during that period than Muslims. Policies that attempt to reduce terrorism by targeting Muslims or individuals of certain racial groups are therefore unlikely, given the statistical frequency of Muslim violence, to be even remotely effective. A vast majority of terrorist incidents in the United States are also committed by US citizens and not by immigrants, despite widely held beliefs that immigration is a significant source of terrorism. [6]

Determining which criteria can be used to identify to terrorists or those with the potential for terrorist activity is challenging. Broadly speaking, the vast majority of twenty-first century terrorist organizations are highly conservative and are seeking to return societies to a more "traditional" state in which a historic balance of power will be restored. Researchers have called this a global "anti-Modernity" movement, which means reestablishing racial or gender-based hierarchies that were once ubiquitous, but that progressive social movements, like those for women's rights, lesbian, gay, bisexual, queer, and transgender (LGBQT) rights, religious freedom, and minority rights, have incrementally worked to dismantle over the past two centuries. [7] Conservative Muslim organizations like the Islamic State would therefore establish a highly fundamentalist version of Islamic practice that restores patriarchic dominance and erases the perceived secularization of their societies. The interpretation of Islam proposed here is not inherently different or less dangerous than the fundamentalist interpretation of the Old or New Testament promoted by Christian extremist organizations like the Ku Klux Klan and the Tripura Front in India. By contrast, from the 1940s through the 1960s, leftist terrorism was more common in the United States, with groups like the Weather Underground committing terrorist attacks against the perceived oppression of a traditionalist, conservative, and racially prejudiced power structure. Between then and the 2010s, the world's many peaceful civil- and social-rights movements succeeded in eroding traditional hierarchies of dominance and this increased the frequency and intensity of conservative, traditionalist extremism.

Terrorist organizations are extremist, but so are nationalist and hate groups promoting ideologies that motivate mass shootings like the one committed by Dylann Roof. The effort to create gun policies that prevent terrorists from obtaining guns should therefore be concurrent with efforts to prevent any form of extremist violence. Generally speaking, such an effort is unlikely to be effective unless the United States found a way to create a gun policy that would prohibit gun ownership for any individual, of any race or background, who espoused extremist views that might motivate violent actions. This would mean prohibiting gun ownership for individuals who hold extreme attitudes about race, religion, gender, and government, as well as prohibiting gun ownership for individuals with extremist attitudes about Islam specifically. While some might agree that banning all extremist gun ownership would be an acceptable, necessary violation of property rights and freedoms, such an effort appears impossible without violating concurrent protections of the right to free speech, assembly, and belief.

Is Gun Violence a Mental-Health Issue?

Another major issue in the 2016 gun debate concerned the alleged intersection between mental health and gun violence. There is a tendency, though largely unsubstantiated, to believe that gun violence and mental health are generally connected. This belief has motivated laws, the first of which was established in 1968, prohibiting individuals who have been committed in mental institutions or have a history of mental-health issues from owning guns. Gun-rights lobbyists and pundits have supported the mental-health assessment of gun violence and have used it to suggest that reducing gun violence can be achieved by strengthening policies that prohibit individuals with mental issues from obtaining guns. This view has been widely embraced in US conservative culture, as evinced by the 2013 article by Ann Coulter, entitled "Guns Don't Kill People, the Mentally Ill Do."[8]

However, scientific studies have failed to demonstrate a positive correlation between mental illness and gun violence. For instance, a 2015 study in the *American Journal of Public Health* found that while there are instances in which mentally ill persons commit gun violence, such as in the widely covered case in Newtown, Connecticut when mentally-ill Adam Lanza killed 20 children and 6 adults at Sandy Hook Elementary school, less than 3 to 5 percent of crimes in the United States involve individuals with diagnosable mental-health issues. Between 2001 and 2010, for instance, fewer than 5 percent of known gun-related killings were committed by individuals diagnosed with mental illness. Studies have shown, unsurprisingly, that mentally ill persons are at significantly higher risk for gun-related suicide.[9]

A 2015 Harvard University study suggested that gun violence is more closely related to anger management than to mental illness. Specifically, researchers found that individuals who owned six or more guns were four times more likely to carry guns outside the home and to be in the high-risk group for anger management issues.

Similarly, the study indicated that as many as 8.9 percent of gun owners self-report behaviors that fit into the psychological definition of "impulsive angry behavior," as well as 1.5 percent of those who carry weapons outside the home.[10] Though corroborating studies are needed, the Harvard University study suggests that restricting gun ownership for individuals with diagnosed mental illness is a far less effective strategy than prohibiting gun ownership for individuals suffering from anger management issues or depression.

Micah L. Issitt

Works Used:

Blake, John. "Does Race Shape Americans' Passion for Guns?" *CNN*. Cable News Network. Oct 12 2014. Web. 28 Dec 2016.

Coulter, Ann. "Guns Don't Kill People, the Mentally Ill Do." *Ann Coulter*. Ann Coulter. Jan 16 2013. Web. 29 Dec 2016.

Frostenson, Sarah. "Most Terrorist Attacks in the US Are Comitted by Americans – Not Foreigners." *Vox*. Vox Media. Sep 9 2016. Web. 28 Dec 2016.

Metzl, Jonathan and Kenneth T. MacLeish. "Mental Illness, Mass Shootings, and the Politics of American Firearms." *American Journal of Public Health*, Vol. 105, No. 2, 2015, 240–49.

Morin, Rich. "The Demographics and Politics of Gun Owning Households." *Pew Research Center*. Pew Foundation. Jul 15 2014. Web. 28 Dec 2016.

O'Brien, Kerry, Forrest, Walter, Lynott, Dermot, and Michael Daly. "Racism, Gun Ownership and Gun Control: Biased Attitudes in US Whites May Influence Policy Decisions." *PLOS*. PLOS. Oct 31 2013. Web. 28 Dec 2016.

Patel, Faiza and Adrienne Tierney. "The Reasons Why Dylann Roof Wasn't Charged with Terrorism." *Just Security*. New York University School of Law. Jul 30 2015. Web. 28 Dec 2016.

Smith, Candace, Kelsey, Adam, and Veronica Stracqualursi. "Trump Says Maybe '2nd Amendment People' Can Stop Clinton's Supreme Court Picks." *ABC News*. ABC. Aug 9 2016. Web. 28 Dec 2016.

Swanson, Jeffery W., et al. "Guns, Impulsive Angry Behavior, and Mental Disorders: Results from the National Comorbidity Survey Replication (NCS-R)." *Behavioral Sciences & the Law*, Vol. 33, Nos. 2-3, June, 2015, 199-212.

Valenti, Jessica. "Why Don't Americans Call Mass Shootings 'Terrorism'? Racism." *The Guardian*. Guardian News and Media. Jun 19 2015. Web. 29 Dec 2016.

"Why Own a Gun? Protection Is Now Top Reason." *Pew Research Center*. Pew Foundation. Mar 12 2013. Web. 28 Dec 2016.

Ye Hee Lee, Michelle. "Giuliani's Claim that 93 Percent of Black Murder Victims Are Killed by Other Blacks." *The Washington Post*. Nash Holdings. Nov 25 2014. Web. 28 Dec 2016.

Zafirovsky, Milan and Daniel G. Rodeheaver. *Modernity and Terrorism*. Boston: Brill Publishers, 2013.

Notes

1. "Why Own a Gun? Protection Is Now Top Reason," *Pew Research*.
2. Morin, "The Demographics and Politics of Gun Owning Households."
3. O'Brien, Forrest, Lynott, and Daly, "Racism, Gun Ownership and Gun Control: Biased Attitudes in US Whites May Influence Policy Decisions."
4. Patel and Tierney, "The Reasons Why Dylann Roof Wasn't Charged With Terrorism."
5. Valenti, "Why Don't Americans Call Mass Shootings 'Terrorism'? Racism."
6. Frostenson, "Most Terrorist Attacks in the US are Committed by Americans— Not Foreigners."
7. Zafirovski and Rodeheaver, *Modernity and Terrorism*.
8. Coulter, "Guns Don't Kill People, the Mentally Ill Do."
9. Metzl and MacLeish, "Mental Illness, Mass Shootings, and the Politics of American Firearms."
10. Swanson, et al. "Guns, Impulsive Angry Behavior, and Mental Disorders: Results from the National Comorbidity Survey Replication (NCS-R)."

Untangling Gun Violence from Mental Illness

By Julie Beck
The Atlantic, June 7, 2016

After a shooting, once the dust has settled, and the initial shock and panic has abated somewhat, fearful minds begin to cast about for explanations. Given the frequency with which gun deaths occur in the United States, "Why did this happen?" and "Who could do something like this?" are questions the country faces with grim regularity.

Unfortunately, a consistent and dangerous narrative has emerged—an explanation all-too-readily at hand when a mass shooting or other violent tragedy occurs: The perpetrator must have been mentally ill.

"We have a strong responsibility as researchers who study mental illness to try to debunk that myth," says Jeffrey Swanson, a professor of psychiatry at Duke University. "I say as loudly and as strongly and as frequently as I can, that mental illness is not a very big part of the problem of gun violence in the United States."

The overwhelming majority of people with mental illnesses are not violent, just like the overwhelming majority of all people are not violent. Only 4 percent of the violence—not just gun violence, but any kind—in the United States is attributable to schizophrenia, bipolar disorder, or depression (the three most-cited mental illnesses in conjunction with violence). In other words, 96 percent of the violence in America has nothing to do with mental illness.

A study from 1998 that followed patients released from psychiatric hospitals found that they were no more prone to violence than other people in their communities—unless they also had a substance abuse problem. So mental illness alone was not a risk factor for violence in this study.

Those are the facts. But cultural narratives are often more powerful than facts, and that 4 percent gets overblown in people's minds.

A new study published in *Health Affairs* shows how the news perpetuates this narrative, with a look at how several prominent newspapers and broadcast networks covered mental illness from 1995 to 2014. More than half of the stories they looked at during that period—55 percent—mentioned violence in conjunction with mental illness. That proportion was pretty much consistent across the 19 years. But stories connecting mental illness with mass shootings specifically increased from 9 percent between 1994 and 2004 to 22 percent between 2005 and 2014.

Perhaps this can be partially attributed to high-profile shootings like the Tucson shooting in 2011, in which the killer did have schizophrenia. "That's an event that is newsworthy, but the fact that it was linked to mental illness is not representative of most people who have schizophrenia, or most violence," says Emma McGinty, the lead author on the study and a professor of health policy at Johns Hopkins University. "[And yet] that link pervades the public psyche."

It pervades so much so that people speculate about killers' mental states, even in the absence of any evidence that they were living with any disorder. For example, in an article about the gunman who recently killed a professor at the University of California, Los Angeles, *New York* magazine writes: "Police do not know for sure yet if Sarkar had a history of mental illness." Why does this particular absence of information bear mentioning? It seems mental illness is so linked to gun violence in people's minds that we have to address it even when it's not there.

And when there is evidence that a killer also happened to have a mental illness—like the pilot who crashed a Germanwings plane in 2015, who had a history of depression—the media seize upon it like a bear trap. "We've got it now! This is what was wrong with him," is the message portrayed.

This is a really tricky needle to thread, because something was clearly wrong with him. Of course someone who is perfectly healthy and well-adjusted in every way would not go out and kill a bunch of people.

"This is one of the hardest distinctions to make," McGinty says. "Anyone who kills someone else in a mass shooting scenario or otherwise is not what we would consider mentally healthy. But that does not mean they have a clinical diagnosis and therefore a treatable mental illness. There could be emotional regulation issues related to anger, for example, which are a separate phenomenon. There could be underlying substance use issues. There could be a whole host of other risk factors for violence going on."

"I think we have a long way to go in terms of brain science to really understand [those] distinctions," adds Ron Honberg, a senior policy advisor at the National Alliance on Mental Illness.

But when the news reinforces these easy narratives, as McGinty's study shows it often does, that can have serious consequences. Other research shows that reading stories about mass shootings by people with mental illnesses makes people feel more negatively toward the mentally ill. This only heightens stigma, which could lead to more people going untreated.

"Do we not risk creating further barriers?" Honberg asks. "People [may] feel like, 'Oh my gosh, if I get identified as having a psychiatric diagnosis, people are going to draw certain conclusions.' It's hard enough to get people to seek help when they need it."

Shootings seem to inevitably lead to people calling for better mental health screenings for guns, or for better mental health care generally. Which would be great, lord knows we need it. But again, better mental health care is not going to have much of an impact on interpersonal violence.

This is a misframing of the issue. There is a compelling reason to adjust policy to better keep some seriously mentally ill people from accessing guns. It's not because they might hurt others, but because they might hurt themselves.

Though big, scary mass shootings get the most attention when it comes to gun violence, 60 percent of deaths caused by firearms are suicides. And another new study in this same issue of *Health Affairs* emphasizes that suicide, not homicide, is the major public health problem for mentally ill people with guns. In it, Swanson and his colleagues looked at 81,704 people getting public health services for schizophrenia, bipolar disorder, or major depressive disorder in two large Florida counties. They tracked these people's death records, as well as whether they were barred from owning guns.

In that group, the rate of people who died by suicide was four times higher than that of the general population. The violent crime rate was just under two times higher. But consider that this is a group of people receiving government care, who "might have other risk factors for violence, including poverty and social disadvantage, unemployment, residential instability, substance use problems, history of violent victimization, exposure to neighborhood violence, or involvement with the criminal justice system," the study reads. So you can't reasonably attribute the higher violent crime rate in this group to mental illness alone.

Maybe also because many people in the group likely lived in poverty, they were less likely to commit suicide by gun than the general population (perhaps they could not afford one). But 72 percent of the people who did kill themselves with a gun were "legally eligible to purchase a gun on the day they used a gun to

> **The news often portrays people with psychiatric disorders as a danger to others, when suicide is the much greater risk.**

end their life," Swanson says. "That suggests a problem with the criteria we have for identifying people at risk." And the 28 percent who were not allowed to purchase guns managed to find one anyway, so the laws we do have are not perfectly enforced.

This is a conversation that plays out time and time again, perhaps because talking about mental illness is easier than talking about the guns.

"It's a big public health opportunity to limit access to guns," Swanson says. And it could make a big difference for suicide attempt survival rates. Among people who've survived a suicide attempt, more than 90 percent do not go on to kill themselves later. But guns are the most common method of suicide, and people who try to kill themselves with a gun usually succeed—85 percent of the time. "They don't get that second chance," Swanson says.

Overall, the study concluded, "[the results] would seem to suggest that suicide, not homicide, should be the crux of gun violence prevention efforts focused on people with serious mental illnesses in public systems of care."

That is not typically the case, though. Both Honberg and Swanson say that in their experience, people talk about increasing gun background checks for people with mental illness in the context of preventing homicide, not suicide. This is a conversation that plays out in the media and among politicians time and time again after a prominent shooting tragedy, perhaps because talking about mental illness is easier than talking about the guns.

"We're a pretty violent society here in America and the conversation really ought to focus on what can be done to make America a less violent society," Honberg says. "But because that discussion is so fraught with emotion and divisiveness and political disagreements, it almost seems like the conversation has devolved to a relatively small subset of people who engage in violence, namely people with mental illness. We can at least agree about what to do with guns and mentally ill people rather than what to do about guns generally. But that's really passing the buck."

Print Citations

CMS: Beck, Julie. "Untangling Gun Violence from Mental Illness." In *The Reference Shelf: Guns in America*, edited by Betsy Maury, 117-20. Ipswich, MA: H.W. Wilson, 2017.

MLA: Beck, Julie. "Untangling Gun Violence from Mental Illness." *The Reference Shelf: Guns in America*. Ed. Betsy Maury. Ipswich: H.W. Wilson, 2017. 117-20. Print.

APA: Beck, J. (2017). Untangling gun violence from mental illness. In Betsy Maury (Ed.), *The reference shelf: Guns in America* (pp. 117-20). Ipswich, MA: H.W. Wilson. (Original work published 2016)

How Racial Prejudice Helps Drive Opposition to Gun Control

By Alexandra Filindra

The Washington Post, June 21, 2016

Last week, Sen. Chris Murphy made a small splash by filibustering on the Senate floor until, he said, Republicans agreed to allow a vote on a modest gun control measure. When the nation has debates like this, commentators often focus either on what was meant by the Second Amendment, or on who supports and who opposes such regulations, examining public opinion divisions along partisan, geographical, or other lines.

My research has identified a different factor, however, that affects public opinion about gun control, and it plays a bigger role than observers often appreciate. That factor is race.

Here's the Racial Breakdown in Gun Ownership and Beliefs About Gun Regulation

Eighty-four percent of gun owners in the United States are white, according to data from the 2012 American National Election Study (ANES). Since whites make up 63 percent of the US population, their representation among gun owners is higher than their share of the general population.

Polls show that whites also make up the majority of those who oppose stricter gun regulations. In a July 2015 Pew poll, for instance, 57 percent of whites said it was more important "to protect the right of Americans to own guns" than to "control gun ownership." Among blacks and Hispanics, that number was just 24 percent. In a 2015 survey conducted through the University of Illinois in Chicago, we asked respondents to rank the importance of key government guarantees. Eighty-five percent of whites ranked the "right to bear arms" among the top three, while only 24 percent of blacks did.

Research finds that support for gun rights is strongest among whites who are racially prejudiced. In a study conducted by Kerry O'Brien and colleagues using data from the ANES, "racial resentment," a common measure of racial prejudice, is correlated with both gun ownership and opposition to gun control. For each 1-point increase on the 5-point racial resentment scale, there is a 50 percent increase in the odds of owning a gun. Similarly, those who score high on racial resentment are

25 percent less likely to support "making it more difficult to buy a gun" than whites who score low. Those results withstand controls for respondents' demographics, political preferences, and values.

Our Research Upheld This Correlation

An experiment I conducted with Noah Kaplan in December 2013 corroborates these survey results. In the experiment, 1,200 whites were randomly divided into two groups. One group was asked to rate the likability and attractiveness of pictures of three white and three black faces.

We told respondents that the purpose of the test was to assess their cognitive ability in rating pictures. We chose to show respondents pictures of both whites and blacks so it would be harder to guess our experiment's actual purpose, which might have encouraged respondents to give the answers they thought to be socially desirable.

We drew the pictures from a commonly used measure of prejudice: the Implicit Association Test. This is a test designed to measure automatic associations in memory between race and positive or negative concepts. These black-and-white pictures are designed to measure race alone, showing only a person's face without any clothes, background, or other markings that could signify class status. The second group did not see or rate any pictures.

Then respondents were asked for their opinions on a number of gun policy proposals. People who saw the pictures were significantly less likely to support gun regulations than those in the control group. From these results, we inferred that when whites are prompted to think about blacks, they are less likely to support gun control. Racial resentment amplified this effect. Among people who saw the pictures, those who scored higher on racial resentment were less likely to support gun control than those whose racial resentment scores were lower.

These studies, of course, do not suggest that every white person who owns a gun is prejudiced against blacks. Rather, they show that those whites who do harbor such prejudices are more likely to own guns and support gun rights.

That's Not Because White Gun Owners Fear Black Violence

Why might these relationships exist? Although 48 percent of gun owners say they own guns for "protection," fear of black crime does not seem to drive the relationship. Fear of crime actually increases support for gun control among whites.

Nor are those whites who support gun rights afraid of violent black protests, as another of my studies finds. In one experiment, conducted in March this year, 806 white respondents were randomly assigned to one of four groups. In each group, they read a short article describing a rally — either a violent or a nonviolent rally by a predominantly white group, the tea party, or a predominantly black group, Black Lives Matter. After reading the story, respondents were asked their views on various gun policy proposals.

Compared with those who read about the white nonviolent rally, respondents were actually more likely to support gun control when they read about a black protest, whether violent or nonviolent. There was no difference in support for gun control between those who read about a violent or a non-violent white rally. So, if anything, the thought of black protesters is more likely to push whites to support gun control.

It's Because of the Symbolic Appeal of Guns to White Americans

The theory of racial resentment, developed by David Sears and Don Kinder, offers an important clue as to what underlies this relationship between prejudice and guns. It goes like this. Unlike "old-fashioned racism," which justifies racial differences in norms and behavior as biological, racially resentful whites believe that many blacks have made a choice to pursue crime and government dependency, behaviors that deviate from traditional American virtues. Some prominent conservative intellectuals have encouraged these beliefs, arguing that blacks have been competing unfairly through affirmative action and that they support color-conscious policies that put whites at a disadvantage. Survey data confirm that 37 percent of whites, and 47 percent of white gun owners, believe that the government "does too much" for blacks.

How is this linked to gun ownership? It may be that the possession of firearms harkens back to the (white) patriots who founded the United States. The "right to bear arms," conjures the image of the virtuous, independent—and white—citizen-soldier, and this gives those white gun owners a feeling of a proud, positive racial identity.

> **Although 48 percent of gun owners say they own guns for "protection," fear of black crime does not seem to drive the relationship.**

In this conception, firearms embody whites' true "American-ness"—and distance them from those perceived to be dependent on the state rather than independent guardians of the Republic, thus violating these "American" values. The symbolism does not quite work for blacks, for whom guns have strong cultural associations not with virtue but with violence.

Since firearms carry such a strong association with notions of virtuous white citizenship, it shouldn't be a surprise that white Americans who feel socially devalued and who attribute that to unfair black gains would see owning firearms as a symbolic way to regain respect and to be seen as noble and virtuous citizens. This also explains the fierce resistance to gun control among many whites: They see gun regulation not as a way to make their community safer, but as an assault on their identity and disrespect to their racial group.

Print Citations

CMS: Filindra, Alexandra. "How Racial Prejudice Helps Drive Opposition to Gun Control." In *The Reference Shelf: Guns in America*, edited by Betsy Maury, 121-24. Ipswich, MA: H.W. Wilson, 2017.

MLA: Filindra, Alexandra. "How Racial Prejudice Helps Drive Opposition to Gun Control." *The Reference Shelf: Guns in America*. Ed. Betsy Maury. Ipswich: H.W. Wilson, 2017. 121-24. Print.

APA: Filindra, A. (2016). How racial prejudice helps drive opposition to gun control. In Betsy Maury (Ed.), *The reference shelf: Guns in America* (pp. 121-24). Ipswich, MA: H.W. Wilson. (Original work published 2016)

The Home-Grown Threat

The Economist, **December 12, 2015**

Despite the attack in San Bernardino, America's defences against jihadism are high.

You do not need to be Donald Trump to be confused by the massacre Syed Rizwan Farook and his Pakistani wife, Tashfeen Malik, carried out in San Bernardino, California, on December 2nd. The couple responsible for the deadliest act of terrorism in America since 2001 were well-educated, affluent and unknown to the police. Mr Farook earned $70,000 a year as a government inspector; his brother served in the navy. Unlike ne'er-do-well European jihadists, with their uncouth accents and mugged-up theology, the killers were quiet, unremarkable middle-class Muslims.

Their target, a get-together of Mr Farook's colleagues at a suburban health centre, was so banal investigators at first suspected the massacre of 14 people was a case of workplace rage. Even the fact that the couple turned out to have kept an arsenal at home and practised on gun ranges was only alarming in retrospect. Millions of Americans do the same. A few minutes before going postal, they dropped off their six-month-old daughter with Mr Farook's mother, claiming to have a doctor's appointment: Mr Farook and Ms Malik were the jihadists next door.

There are two starkly opposed ways of understanding this banality. The first, exemplified by President Barack Obama, is to find it almost reassuring. In an address from the Oval Office on December 6th he said the attack reflected America's success in preventing more spectacular terrorist violence. While promising one or two security measures—including checks on the fiancé visa on which Ms Malik entered America—he also urged Americans to see the killing in the context of an already violent society: "As we've become better at preventing complex, multifaceted attacks like 9/11, terrorists turned to less complicated acts of violence like the mass-shootings that are all too common." The best way to foil them, Mr Obama added, was to keep calm and carry on. "Our success won't depend on tough talk, or abandoning our values, or giving into fear. That's what groups like [Islamic State] are hoping for."

The alternative, demonstrated by Mr Trump, is to conclude that, since such Muslim maniacs are hard to detect, all Muslims must be considered suspect. "We have to look at mosques. We have no choice. We have to see what is happening because something is happening in there. Man, is there anger!" mused the front-runner for the Republican presidential nomination. His solution was a perfect rebuke to Mr

Obama: Mr Trump called "for a total and complete shutdown of Muslims entering the United States until our country's representatives can figure out what is going on".

> **By far the most important reason, however, is that American Muslims are less interested in being radicalised than their European counterparts.**

The facts are with the president. Since 9/11, over 400,000 people have been killed by gunfire in America and 45 by jihadist violence, of whom half died in two shootings: one carried out by a Muslim army doctor in Texas in 2009, the other in San Bernardino. France has so far suffered seven fatal jihadist attacks this year, costing 150 lives; America has suffered nine at home in 14 years. And though the government has raised its threat levels, fearing San Bernardino could augur an uptick, that is partly a matter of due diligence. "I see the threat as being relatively consistent since 9/11," says Raymond Kelly, who served as New York's police commissioner between 2002 and 2013, and now works for a corporate snooper, K2 Intelligence.

Three things account for America's relative security. The first is its distance from the Middle East; the second is decent law enforcement, especially by the FBI, which since 2001 has partly turned itself into the internal spy agency America lacked. Its counter-terrorism staff, whose number has grown by 2,000, are investigating links to IS in 50 states. By far the most important reason, however, is that American Muslims are less interested in being radicalised than their European counterparts.

They are richer, better educated and altogether better integrated into the mainstream. Though less than 1% of America's population, they account for 10% of its doctors; in 2011, less than half said that most of their closest friends were Muslims. Plainly, IS, which has flooded the internet with jihadist propaganda, represents a new test to that moderation. Yet, as a rule, American Muslims are probably less tempted by a genocidal medieval revival act than any others in the West. While more than 5,000 Europeans have joined IS, fewer than 250 Americans are thought to have tried to—of whom, estimates Peter Bergen, author of a forthcoming book on American jihadists, only two dozen succeeded.

This also makes American Muslims unusually likely to report suspected jihadists to the police. According to Mohamed Magid, a Virginia-based imam who has advised the administration on radicalisation, 42% of the jihadist plots rumbled since 2001 were reported by suspicious Muslims. That includes a recent case within his own

> **While more than 5,000 Europeans have joined IS, fewer than 250 Americans are thought to have tried to—of whom, estimates Peter Bergen, author of a forthcoming book on American jihadists, only two dozen succeeded.**

congregation, in which the parents of a 16-year-old youth, Ali Amin, reported his interest in IS. He was sentenced in August to 11 years in prison after pleading guilty to fund-raising for IS and helping another American teenager, Reza Niknejad, join it. Mr Amin was radicalised online by IS agents in Canada and Britain. "It doesn't matter where the recruiter is so long as there is internet," said Mr Magid. "But thank God his parents came forward."

That is why Mr Trump's demagoguery, occasioned as much by a bad poll for the blow-hard in Iowa as the massacre in California, is so dangerous, as well as wrong. Americans are lucky. Their defences against jihadism are high. But that is provided Muslims are manning them, which Mr Trump has already made less likely.

At an Islamic Centre in Jersey City, whose large Muslim population Mr Trump had previously accused, mendaciously, of celebrating 9/11, people are rattled. "When we heard about the Paris and California attacks, first thing that comes to our mind is, 'Oh God, please don't let it be a Muslim'," says Ahmed Shedeed, the centre's president. "The good thing is we look like Latinos," he adds. Given how Mr Trump once denigrated Mexicans as rapists, that shows how his campaign has moved on.

Print Citations

CMS: "The Home-Grown Threat: Despite the Attack in San Bernardino, America's Defences against Jihadism Are High." In *The Reference Shelf: Guns in America*, edited by Betsy Maury, 125-27. Ipswich, MA: H.W. Wilson, 2017.

MLA: "The Home-Grown Threat: Despite the Attack in San Bernardino, America's Defences against Jihadism Are High." *The Reference Shelf: Guns in America*. Ed. Betsy Maury. Ipswich: H.W. Wilson, 2017. 125-27. Print.

APA: The Economist. (2017). The home-grown threat: Despite the attacks in San Bernardino, America's defences against jihadism are high. In Betsy Maury (Ed.), *The reference shelf: Guns in America* (pp. 125-27). Ipswich, MA: H.W. Wilson. (Original work published 2015)

What Public Health Researchers Want You to Know about Gun Control

By Ziming Xuan and Sandro Galen
The Conversation, October 3, 2015

Q: How common are mass shootings in the US? Do you consider gun violence a public health issue?

Ziming Xuan: President Obama Thursday night spoke about the "routine" nature of mass shooting in our country. Gun violence is often among the leading causes of death (homicides and suicides) and non-fatal injuries among youth, and affects families and communities across the US.

Gun violence has created a major and unique public health problem for the US, compared to other developed countries. In order to protect youth, the governments and adults in other developed countries such as France have made it difficult for youth to access handguns. However, a recent study showed that about a quarter of US adolescents reported they had easy access to a gun in their home. Meanwhile, the majority of young respondents told researchers they wished to live in a society where it is impossible for teens to obtain guns.

Sandro Galea: There have been 45 school shootings in America this year alone. Mass shootings have been occurring with regularity in the US for years now. More than 32,000 people die from firearms every year, as many as die from car accidents. This is clearly a public health issue, and one with a solution—the control of widespread gun availability.

Q: If the US committed to ending mass shootings, what does research suggest would be the best strategy?

Sandro Galea: Control over availability of weapons, as has been done in countries like Australia, has been shown to work.

Ziming Xuan: The best and longest-lasting approach involves comprehensive policy changes. We must also shift the community norms to be more consistent with the public health nature of this problem.

Q: Oregon—where Thursday's shootings took place—is one of seven states that allow guns on college campuses. What impact will 'campus carry' laws have on gun violence?

Sandro Galea: Wider availability of firearms is associated with more firearm-related injury. Allowing guns on campus is the wrong strategy toward reducing firearm injury.

Ziming Xuan: Published research has shown that states with weak laws and more guns are associated with more gun violence in the forms of suicide, homicides and other injuries and accidents.

Q: What else should people know to understand gun violence in the US?

Ziming Xuan: Considering the magnitude of the gun violence problem in the US, gun-related research is limited in part because there is virtually no funding from the federal government to advance our understanding about the nature and mechanism of gun violence or to identify and evaluate effective prevention strategies.

Parents definitely need to teach their children to be responsible with risky and lethal products such as alcohol, guns, cars and so on. However, parents sometimes do not understand fully about child and youth development, impulsiveness or curiosity. A recent study shows that what parents report about their children's access to guns often contradicts children's reports; the kids reveal that they know the location of guns in the house and have handled the gun, while parents reported they did not. For injury prevention, it is far more effective and long-lasting to change the environment by changing modifiable policies and norms than to change the child.

> **Meanwhile, the majority of young respondents told researchers they wished to live in a society where it is impossible for teens to obtain guns.**

Sandro Galea: Firearm deaths are driven principally by availability of firearms. While frequently after these events we link them to mental illness, the evidence is very clear that this is a negligible part of the problem. People with mental illness are much more likely to be victims than perpetrators of firearm violence.

Print Citations

CMS: Xuan, Ziming, and Sandro Galen. "What Public Health Researchers Want You to Know about Gun Control." In *The Reference Shelf: Guns in America*, edited by Betsy Maury, 128-29. Ipswich, MA: H.W. Wilson, 2017.

MLA: Xuan, Ziming, and Sandro Galen. "What Public Health Researchers Want You to Know about Gun Control." *The Reference Shelf: Guns in America*. Ed. Betsy Maury. Ipswich: H.W. Wilson, 2017. 128-29. Print.

APA: Xuan, Z., & S. Galen (2016). What public health researchers want you to know about gun control. In Betsy Maury (Ed.), *The reference shelf: Guns in America* (pp. 128-29). Ipswich, MA: H.W. Wilson. (Original work published 2015)

Blaming Gun Violence on the Mentally Ill Is Easy, but Ignorant

By Jason Powers
The Huffington Post, October 8, 2016

A meme that circulated recently on social media suggested that the days of going to our comedians for levity and our politicians for public policy are over. According to the post, we now get our belly laughs from Donald Trump and discussions of serious social issues from the likes of John Oliver.

As a physician treating the mentally ill and addicted, this was never more evident to me than on Sunday, when Oliver, on his HBO show *Last Week Tonight*, addressed the sad state of mental health care in the United States. Oh sure, the British-born comic made the subject plenty funny—the system, he said, is a "cluster f—, except that's an insult to cluster f—-s"—but he hit many nails directly on their heads.

Oliver reported that the inadequacy of the mental health system to meet the needs of an estimated 43.8 million mentally ill Americans, of which about 10 million, or roughly the population of Greece, suffer from serious psychiatric conditions, is not a subject that anyone wishes to discuss ... until there is a mass shooting, such as the recent tragedy in Roseburg, Oregon. "Perhaps the clearest sign of just how little we want to talk about mental health," Oliver said, "is that one of the only times it's actively brought up is, as we've seen yet again this week, in the aftermath of a mass shooting as a means of steering the conversation away from gun control."

While I will not address the pros and cons of gun control in the U.S., it is true that the three presidential candidates quoted in the segment certainly sounded gung-ho on the issue of treating the mentally ill. "Do we need to do a better job in mental health?" asked Mike Huckabee, former governor of Arkansas. "You bet we do." (Of course, Oliver then pointed out that Arkansas, under Huckabee, had received a D- grade from the National Alliance on Mental Illness for its treatment of the mentally ill.)

"It seems there is nothing like a mass shooting to suddenly spark political interest in mental health," Oliver said. He then pointed out that the aftermath of gun violence is perhaps the worst time to talk about mental health when you consider that the large majority of those with psychological disorders are not violent. In fact, media reports connecting violence to mental illness only increase the stigma directed toward the mentally ill. A 2013 study conducted by researchers at the Johns Hopkins Bloomberg School of Public Health found that news reports about a mass shooting immediately increased readers' negative impressions about people with mental illnesses, with more than half stating that those with serious mental illness were likely to be dangerous.

In a separate public opinion survey conducted by the same researchers, almost half of the respondents believed that people with serious mental illness are more dangerous than members of the general population and most said they were unwilling to have a person with a serious mental illness as a coworker or a neighbor.

"Treatment" Left to Jailers

How do we address the inadequacy of a mental health system in which, Oliver reports, there are 10 times more mentally ill people being "treated" in jails and prisons (2 million) than there are in state-funded psychiatric treatment?

A couple of possibilities were raised on *Last Week Tonight*. Establishing more crisis intervention units within local police departments would be a good first step, since police are often the first to confront a person manifesting symptoms of serious mental illness, and these encounters can end badly. (Oliver cited one report demonstrating that half of the incidents in which police used deadly force were calls involving a mentally ill person.) Only 15 percent of all law enforcement jurisdictions have crisis intervention programs, let alone special units, and crisis intervention training is voluntary.

The report also addressed Assertive Community Treatment (ACT) programs, in which the mentally ill can continue living in the community with the assistance of social workers who help patients attend to their treatment and daily needs. Despite the success of these programs, and the fact that they largely pay for themselves, they are in danger in many states due to budget cuts and issues relating to Medicaid reimbursement.

So, if the need for better mental health care is anything more than a talking point to deflect attention away from gun control, there is plenty to discuss. Because, in reality, the two subjects have surprisingly little to do with each other.

Vast Majority of Mentally Ill Will Never Be Violent

Trump blamed mental illness for the tragic loss of life in Oregon. "This isn't guns; this is about mental illness," the leading GOP presidential candidate said on ABC's *This Week*. "You have sick people in this country and throughout the world, and you're always going to have difficulty." And while on the face of it, you don't have to be a doctor to know that no one is his right mind would take the lives of nine innocent people, the vast majority of mentally ill people are not violent and never will be. Mental health disorders are much more strongly linked to self-harm than to violence against others.

Oliver cited "one study that found that fewer than 5 percent of 120,000 gun-related killings were committed by people diagnosed with mental illness." That comprehensive study was done by Vanderbilt University researchers Jonathan Metzl and Kenneth MacLeish, who analyzed data and literature linking guns and mental illness over 40 years. The researchers concluded that it's not the stereotypical "violent madman," the young, white, angry male, whom we need to fear.

"You're far more likely to be shot by your neighbor or your cousin or disgruntled brother-in-law than by some crazed stranger," said Metzl, the study's lead author. "[There's this] fear of the unknown stranger . . . some crazy person who is going to come and shoot you. But if you look at the research . . . you're far more likely to be shot by someone you know."

"We should set our gun policies based on the everyday shootings, not the sensational shootings," Metzl said. "The mentally ill across the board are 60 percent to 120 percent more likely than the aver-

> A 2013 study conducted by researchers at the Johns Hopkins Bloomberg School of Public Health found that news reports about a mass shooting immediately increased readers' negative impressions about people with mental illnesses, with more than half stating that those with serious mental illness were likely to be dangerous.

age person to be the victims of violent crime, not the perpetrators. People with severe mental illness often are homeless or talking to themselves, odd in a certain kind of way, and they become targets. We need to pay much more attention to mental health systems. How do people get care? Do they have health insurance, is there follow-up, is there medication available to them?"

The clincher: "It's a failure of the system that becomes represented as a failure of the individual."

Think Risky Behavior, Not Mental Illness

What *does* predict gun violence? A history of violent behavior, a history of childhood abuse, substance use at the time of an emotionally charged event and the availability of a firearm are all better risk indicators for violent behavior than psychiatric diagnoses. In addition, substance abuse appears to be a major predictor of violence whether it occurs along with a concurrent mental illness or not.

Dr. Jeffrey Swanson, a professor of psychiatry and behavioral sciences at the Duke University School of Medicine and an expert on the connection between violence and mental illness, said in a recent interview with ProPublica, "the risk factors for a mass shooting are shared by a lot of people who aren't going to do it . . . if you paint the picture of a young, isolated, delusional young man . . . that probably describes thousands of other young men." He cites a 2001 study of mass shooters that found three out of four had no psychiatric history and only 6% were judged to have been psychotic at the time of the mass murder.

Swanson says that even if schizophrenia, bipolar disorder and depression were cured, violent crime in this nation would decrease by only about 4 percent.

So making the mentally ill scapegoats for gun violence may be convenient, but it's flat-out wrong and won't make anyone safer.

Print Citations

CMS: Powers, Jason. "Blaming Gun Violence on the Mentally Ill Is Easy, but Ignorant." In *The Reference Shelf: Guns in America*, edited by Betsy Maury, 130-32. Ipswich, MA: H.W. Wilson, 2017.

MLA: Powers, Jason. "Blaming Gun Violence on the Mentally Ill Is Easy, but Ignorant." *The Reference Shelf: Guns in America*. Ed. Betsy Maury. Ipswich: H.W. Wilson, 2017. 130-32. Print.

APA: Powers, J. (2017). Blaming gun violence on the mentall ill is easy, but ignorant. In Betsy Maury (Ed.), *The reference shelf: Guns in America* (pp. 130-32). Ipswich, MA: H.W. Wilson. (Original work published 2016)

Fixation on Terrorism Blinds US to Domestic Threats to National Security

By Michael A. Cohen
World Politics Review, January 13, 2016

Paul Ryan, the speaker of the US House of Representatives, is none too impressed with President Barack Obama's plan to curtail gun violence in America by tightening purchasing requirements through executive order.

In an interview with Katie Couric of Yahoo News, Ryan complained that "a week [when] we . . . talk about gun control is a week we're not talking about our failure to confront [the self-described Islamic State] fully, the failure to take care of the threat that's on our doorstep."

To call the Islamic State, rather than guns, "the threat that's on our doorstep" is rather extraordinary, since gun violence takes more American lives each day— roughly 80—than the Islamic State has in its history. And as if the loss of 30,000 American lives each year weren't grim enough, gun violence also costs the United States approximately $229 billion annually, according to research done by *Mother Jones*.

Yet, Ryan believes the president's priorities are backward: He "should put as much effort into going after homegrown jihadis and going after terrorist infiltration of our refugee network and going after defeating [the Islamic State] than he is in trying to frustrate the law-abiding citizens' Second Amendment rights."

This, too, is an odd statement at a moment when a group of legally armed Americans with a clear anti-government agenda are currently exercising their Second Amendment rights by occupying the headquarters of a wildlife refuge in Oregon and threatening violence against law enforcement officials if they try to dislodge them. While these self-declared "militia members" are not terrorists—at least not yet—it suggests that the threat of homegrown violence comes as much from other Americans as from foreign jihadis.

Indeed, Ryan's words are perhaps the best possible reminder of America's bizarre and debilitating fixation on terrorism. It's also a reminder that terrorism has become seemingly the only word in America's national security debates that can generate enough urgency to get a federal response.

But to be clear, it's not just any terrorism that has this effect, only jihadi terrorism.

Consider, for example, that in the months before the mass shooting in San Bernardino, which was quickly defined as a terrorist attack because of the connection between the shooters and the Islamic State, there were several other shocking attacks in the United States.

Over the summer, a white supremacist named Dylann Roof entered an African-American church in Charleston, South Carolina, and massacred 9 people. His goal was to spark a race war between whites and blacks. In November, a gunman in Colorado Springs shot up a Planned Parenthood clinic because, as he put it, "I am a warrior for the babies."

Though both attacks generated shock and outrage, they also triggered a national debate over whether they should even be described as terrorism. The answer is quite clearly yes.

And then there's the situation in Oregon, in which one of the key protagonists is Ammon Bundy, the son of a Nevada rancher who has been in conflict with the US government for decades over his illegal use of federal land for cattle grazing. Back in 2013, when federal law officials tried to seize some of Bundy's cattle—and enforce the numerous court decisions that that have gone against the rancher over the years—they were forced to stand down by Bundy's armed supporters, who had gathered at the ranch. Two of those individuals would later gun down two Las Vegas police officers and declare their actions the beginning of a political revolution, yet another example of domestic terrorism.

As the *New York Times* wrote over the weekend, this kind of situation should not come as a surprise. Back in 2009, the Department of Homeland Security drafted a report warning of a "growing anti-government movement" and the recruiting of veterans returning from Iraq and Afghanistan that could "lead to the potential emergence of terrorist groups or lone-wolf extremists."

The report generated a furious backlash from Republicans in Congress, who questioned why the government was looking at domestic actors and not focusing their attention on foreign jihadi terrorists. DHS head Janet Napolitano retracted the report and disbanded the office at DHS looking at domestic radicalization.

> **If the US is so concerned about terrorism as a nation, why is it ignoring non-Islamic domestic terrorism?**

Yet, according to a 2013 report produced by the Combating Terrorism Center at West Point, "Right-wing extremists have launched an average of 330 attacks a year and killed about 250 people between 2002 and 2011." That's more Americans than have been killed by al-Qaida or the Islamic State in the same period. If the US is so concerned about terrorism as a nation, why is it ignoring non-Islamic domestic terrorism?

Increasingly, the recourse to guns to settle disputes and manifest opposition to government policies has become a persistent feature of America's social and political landscape. From that perspective, how is gun violence not included in discussions of direct threats to US national security? The answer lies, in part, in the fact that gun violence—and the relative ease with which Americans can buy guns, which Obama is seeking to tighten up—are not even considered national security issues.

But in an era of largely non-existent or minimal foreign threats in which the US faces no true military competitor, Americans need to rethink what national security means. If gun violence is reducing economic output by more than $200 billion a year, that affects America's national power and its broader economic competitiveness. The same could be said of public health challenges like obesity, which costs the US economy an estimated $147 billion, and crumbling national infrastructure, the costs of which could run into the trillions of dollars. This is also true of poor educational performance compared to other OECD countries; declining innovation capacity; arrested social mobility; and rising inequality, all of which have significant economic effects. So if Americans do wish to address real national security threats, they should be paying more attention to these issues and worrying less about the minimal threat of jihadi terrorism.

There are clear reasons why Paul Ryan would rather talk about the Islamic State than guns, and it has mostly to do with domestic politics. But let there be no doubt, it has nothing to do with national security.

Print Citations

CMS: Cohen, Michael A. "Fixation on Terrorism Blinds U.S. to Domestic Threats to National Security." In *The Reference Shelf: Guns in America*, edited by Betsy Maury, 134-36. Ipswich, MA: H.W. Wilson, 2017.

MLA: Cohen, Michael A. "Fixation on Terrorism Blinds U.S. to Domestic Threats to National Security." *The Reference Shelf: Guns in America*. Ed. Betsy Maury. Ipswich: H.W. Wilson, 2017. 134-36. Print.

APA: Cohen, M.A. (2017). Fixation on terrorism blinds U.S. to domestic threats to national security. In Betsy Maury (Ed.), *The reference shelf: Guns in America* (pp. 134-36). Ipswich, MA: H.W. Wilson. (Original work published 2016)

How to Prevent Gun Deaths? Where Experts and the Public Agree

By Quoctrung Bui and Margot Sanger-Katz
The New York Times, January 10, 2017

We conducted a survey on 29 gun control ideas, looking for the intersection of effectiveness and popularity.

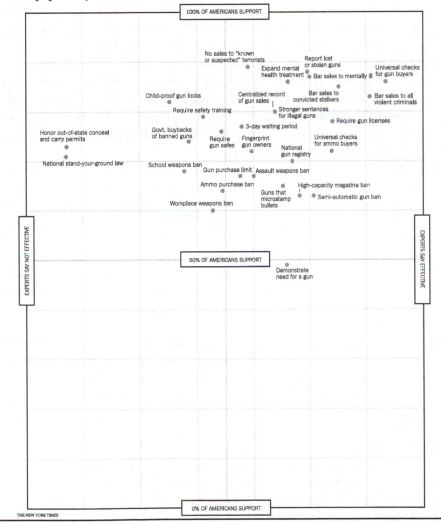

The mass shooting at the Fort Lauderdale airport in Florida last week shows how much the conversation around gun violence has changed since the presidential election.

Five people were killed, and many others were injured; a few months ago, such carnage would have prompted new calls for more restrictions on guns. But Republicans are preparing to control the White House along with Congress. Donald J. Trump has promised to roll back gun restrictions. The most prominent gun measure currently before Congress is one that would allow people with concealed-weapon permits from one state to carry their weapons to other states.

The concealed carry legislation is one of many gun measures that policy makers have debated in recent years. Backers of those ideas, whether the emphasis is gun rights or gun control, often say the intent is to make Americans safer. We've wondered whether the various ideas politicians talk about would work, and whether the public would support them. In June, we asked Morning Consult, a media and polling firm, to survey two groups: some of the country's leading experts on gun violence, and a representative sample of the American electorate.

Our expert survey asked dozens of social scientists, lawyers and public health officials how effective each of 29 policies would be in reducing firearm homicide deaths, regardless of their political feasibility or cost. Policies deemed both effective and popular appear in the upper-right corner of the matrix. Less popular, less effective measures fall lower down and to the left.

The two policies ranked most effective were those requiring all sellers to run background checks on anyone who buys a gun, and barring gun sales to people convicted of violent misdemeanors, including domestic assaults. The experts were more skeptical of other much-debated proposals, including a national gun registry and an assault weapons ban. The idea of requiring states to honor out-of-state concealed weapon permits was ranked low.

The academics in our panel — many of the country's best empirical researchers on gun policy — were far more likely than the general public to support gun control. But nearly all of the policies that experts think could work have widespread support from the general public.

While Americans remain sharply divided in their overall view of the tension between gun control and gun rights, individual proposals are widely favored. The most popular measures in our survey — policies like universal background checks and keeping guns from convicted stalkers — were supported by more than 85 percent of registered voters. Even the least popular idea, a law that would limit gun sales to people who had to demonstrate a "genuine need" for the weapon, was favored by nearly 50 percent.

"We think of guns being an incredibly controversial topic, but what your polling shows and ours has shown is there's a whole lot of gun policies that really aren't controversial," said Daniel Webster, a professor and director of the Johns Hopkins center for gun policy and research.

Public support, of course, doesn't always translate into legislative action. The Republican Congress, like Mr. Trump, has shown little appetite for measures that would curb gun rights.

What Does Trump Support?

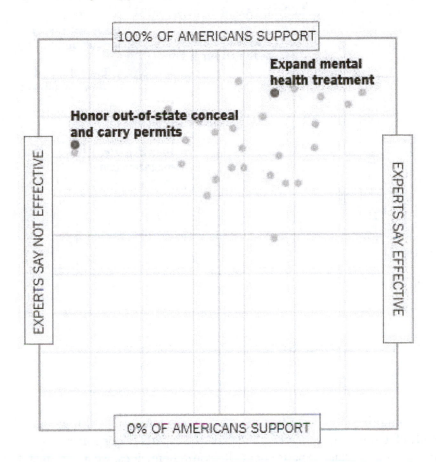

Historically, Mr. Trump has expressed support for some of the more popular measures on our matrix. But once he entered the presidential race, he came out strongly against changes that might limit gun rights for most Americans. He has said that he supports nationalizing concealed carry permits, and that he wants to lift restrictions on carrying guns in places like schools or military bases.

The concealed carry bill was one of the first introduced in the new Congress. The bill, filed by Richard Hudson, a Republican representative from North Carolina, would require states to honor out-of-state permits to carry a concealed weapon even if the standards for obtaining them differ, just as states honor driver's licenses from other states.

On our matrix, it is one of the worst-performing ideas. Our panel of experts did not think it would be effective in reducing gun homicides, though a majority of Americans said they'd support it.

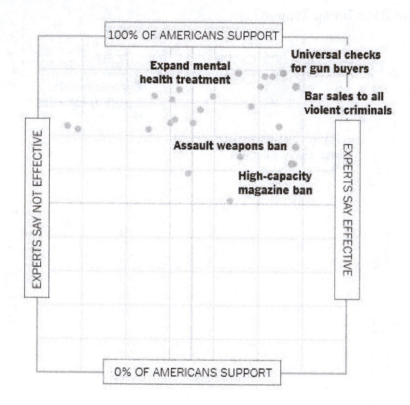

Mr Trump has also advocated more treatment for people with mental illness. That idea fared better among the public and the experts in our surveys.

In addition to asking experts about all firearm homicides, we asked them to rate the same set of policies according to their effectiveness in reducing mass shootings, which make up around 1 percent of gun homicide deaths. Many of their favored policies stayed the same, but a few changed.

Bans on assault weapons and large-capacity ammunition magazines, or limitations on ammunition purchases, would have a greater effect on mass shootings than on routine gun violence, according to the survey. Those rules wouldn't necessarily reduce the number of mass shootings, the experts said, but could lower the death toll when they occur.

Measures Supported by Academics Opposed to Gun Control

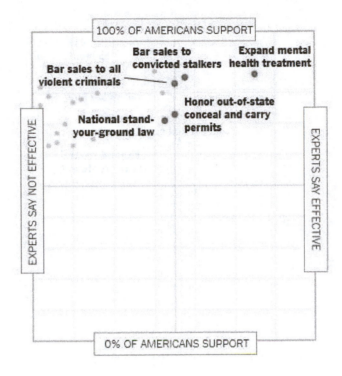

Most of our experts generally favor gun control policies. Only five said they oppose them, and these five rated nearly every policy option as less effective than their colleagues did. But there were still some policies they thought would reduce gun homicides, including expanded screening and treatment of mental illness, and restrictions on gun sales to people convicted of stalking.

Our gun experts who were opposed to gun control tended to particularly oppose blanket policies. "The essence of a ban is it applies to everyone equally, at least theoretically," said Gary Kleck, an emeritus professor of criminology and criminal justice at Florida State University. "But in practice, criminals, being criminals, don't obey the law."

We also asked the National Rifle Association for its favored gun control policies and its thoughts on our results, but the group declined to comment.

Things Law Enforcement Likes

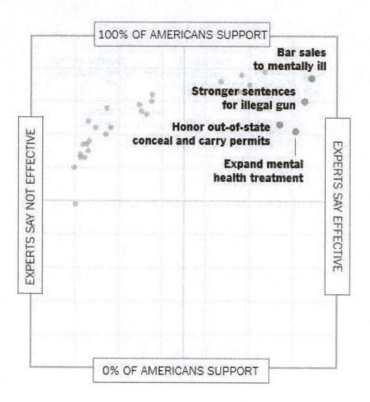

We asked the membership of two groups of law enforcement professionals to answer our survey (their responses were not combined with those of the academic experts). Just under 100 police officers and chiefs responded, representing only a small percentage of the law enforcement community.

In general, the participating law enforcement professionals expressed more support than the academics for measures that would encourage the use of guns by civilians to defend themselves against crime. They gave higher ratings on stand-your-ground laws and the concealed carry measure, for example. They were far more wary than the academics of measures that involved banning categories of firearms or restricting where individuals can carry guns.

Our sample mixes the two groups of law enforcement professionals, which may obscure differences among them. Previous research has shown that police chiefs tend to be more supportive of policies that restrict gun access, while rank-and-file police officers tend to favor more gun rights.

Other Ideas

In interviews, we asked some of our experts for safety ideas that weren't included in our survey.

A few pointed to strategies that wouldn't involve new legislation or regulation, particularly for gang-related gun homicides, which are far more common than mass shootings. Studies have shown that a few programs that focus on community outreach can reduce gun violence in cities. Expanding such programs wouldn't require new laws, just more funding.

There were also some policies that we didn't ask about. We didn't ask about a ban on all handguns, which Washington, D.C., and Chicago have tried. Nor did we ask about barring gun sales to people with a history of alcohol-related offenses, like D.U.I.s. We didn't ask about lifting restrictions on carrying guns on military bases or near schools, which Mr. Trump has endorsed. And we didn't ask about a measure, recently passed in a few states, that would allow law enforcement officials or family members to seek a kind of restraining order from a judge to temporarily confiscate guns from a person who appears to be in crisis.

What Works and Doesn't Work in Reducing Gun Deaths

Suggested Policy	Effectiveness	Public Support
Requiring all sellers to run background checks on anyone who buys a gun.	7.3	86%
Preventing sales of all firearms to people who have been convicted of violent misdemeanors, including domestic assaults.	7.1	83%
Preventing sales of all firearms to people who have been convicted of stalking another person	6.5	85%
Requiring all gun owners to possess a license for their firearm.	6.4	78%
Requiring all sellers to run background checks on anyone who buys ammunition.	6.4	72%
Banning the sale and ownership of all semi-automatic and automatic firearms.	6.1	63%
Preventing sales of all firearms to people who have been reported as dangerous to law enforcement by a mental health provider.	6.0	87%
Requiring all owners to report lost or stolen firearms.	6.0	88%
Banning the sale and ownership of all ammunition magazines with a capacity greater than 10 bullets.	5.8	63%
Requiring that all firearms be recorded in a national registry.	5.7	70%
Expanding screening and treatment for the mentally ill.	5.6	86%
Requiring that all gun buyers demonstrate a a "genuine need" for a gun, such as a law enforcement job or hunting.	5.6	49%
Requiring all guns to microstamp each bullet with a mark that uniquely matches the gun and bullet.	5.5	65%
Increasing minimum penalties for people found possessing firearms illegally.	5.4	80%

Suggested Policy	Effectiveness	Public Support
Requiring gun dealers to keep, retain and report all gun records and sales to the Federal government.	5.4	80%
Banning the sale and ownership of assault rifles or similar firearms.	5.0	67%
Requiring all gun owners to register their fingerprints.	5.0	72%
Preventing sales of all firearms and ammunition to anyone considered to be a "known or suspected terrorist" by the F.B.I.	4.9	89%
Requiring a mandatory waiting period of three days after gun is purchased before it can be taken home.	4.8	77%
Limiting the number of guns that can be purchased to one per month.	4.8	67%
Limiting the amount of ammunition you can purchase within a given time period.	4.4	64%
Requiring that all gun owners store their guns in a safe storage unit.	4.4	76%
Banning firearms from all workplace settings nationally.	4.3	60%
Requiring that gun buyers complete safety training and a test for their specific firearm.	4.1	79%
Implementing a national "buy-back" program for all banned firearms and magazines, where the government pays people to turn in illegal guns.	3.9	74%
Banning firearms from schools and college campuses nationally.	3.8	68%
Requiring that all gun owners store their guns with childproof locks.	3.5	82%
Requiring every state to honor out-of-state permits to carry a concealed weapon.	1.7	73%
Authorizing stand-your-ground laws nationally that allow people to defend themselves using lethal force without needing to retreat first.	1.7	71%

How We Made Our Matrix

To build a list of possible policies, we consulted the academic literature on laws from American states and foreign countries and spoke with advocates for gun rights and gun control. Both surveys were conducted in June of last year.

For our measure of popularity, Morning Consult conducted an internet survey of 1,975 voters, who were asked whether they approved of the possible laws.

For our effectiveness survey, we asked experts in gun policy to evaluate each idea on a scale of 1 to 10, according to how effective they thought it would be in reducing fatalities. We asked the experts to ignore considerations of political or legal feasibility.

Our expert panel consisted of 32 current or retired academics in criminology, public health and law, who have published extensively in peer-reviewed academic journals on gun policy. We know our sample is small and may not include every expert that readers would like consulted. But we feel it represents a useful, if imperfect, measure of what people steeped in the research think might save lives.

The panel of academics included: Cathy Barber, Magdalena Cerdá, Jay Corzine, John Donohue, Laura Dugan, Liza H. Gold, David Hemenway, David Kennedy, Louis Klarevas, Gary Kleck, David Kopel, Tomislav Kovandzic, Adam Lankford, John Lott, Jonathan Metzl, Matthew Miller, Carlisle E. Moody, Andrew Papachristos, Charles Ransford, Peter Reuter, Mark Rosenberg, Robert J. Sampson, Michael Siegel, Gary Slutkin, Robert Spitzer, Stephen P. Teret, George E. Tita, Eugene Volokh, Daniel Webster, April Zeoli and others.

Special thanks to the Fraternal Order of Police and the Major Cities Chiefs Association for distributing the survey to their membership.

Print Citations

CMS: Bui, Quoctrung and Margot Sanger-Katz "How to Prevent Gun Deaths? Where Experts and the Public Agree" In *The Reference Shelf: Guns in America*, edited by Betsy Maury 137-45, Ipswich, MA: Salem Press, 2016

MLA: Bui, Quoctrung and Margot Sanger-Katz "How to Prevent Gun Deaths? Where Experts and the Public Agree" In *The Reference Shelf: Guns in America*. Ed. Betsy Maury. Ipswich: Salem Press, 2016. 137-45. Print.

APA: Bui, Q and M. Sanger-Katz How to Prevent Gun Deaths? Where Experts and the Public Agree. In Betsy Maury (Ed.) *The Reference Shelf: Guns in America* (pp. 132-45). Ipswich, MA: Salem. (Original work published in 2017)

5
The Future of Guns in America

Mary Strohmeyer displays a Donald Trump campaign bumper sticker November 5, 2016 in Lancaster, Pennsylvania.

Alternative Futures in Gun Policy

The shocking and tragic Sandy Hook Elementary School shooting in which a 20-year-old man, Adam Lanza, armed with legally purchased weapons killed twenty 6- and 7-year-olds and several of their teachers, is the type of event that some Americans hoped would galvanize the public in support of gun control. Mass shootings were the turning point for gun policy in the United Kingdom and Australia, but, in a nation that has embraced gun ownership as a symbol of American exceptionalism, identity, and personal freedom, even a crime so horrifying was insufficient to create a mandate for legislation. Some called for bans on assault weapons, which Lanza used in his attack, while others argued for stronger policies on personal arsenals (as Lanza's mother had a personal arsenal in her home) and a smaller minority argued for more comprehensive gun control across the board. Gun-rights groups proposed a different scenario; that if the Sandy Hook teachers had been legally armed, and had carried their guns in the school, or if better mental-health screening methods had been in place, the tragedy could have been prevented. Proponents of this idea then attacked federal laws prohibiting guns from being carried on school grounds, argued that liberal policies on mental health were one of the greatest threats to controlling gun violence, pushed for more permissive laws allowing individuals to carry loaded weapons, and fought against legislation to ban assault rifles on the basis that a teacher with an assault rifle might prevent another school shooting.[1]

The US legislature did nothing after the Sandy Hook massacre as neither argument—that fewer guns or banning certain types of weapons could prevent mass shootings, or that citizens with guns and mental-health screenings would prevent violence—gained enough support, in the legislature, to establish new laws. The failure of the legislature demonstrates the severe ideological polarization in the United States government, a product of many interrelated factors (lobbying, gerrymandering, etc.) that leads to the amplification of extreme viewpoints and reduces representation for the majority of Americans. Most Americans, while they care about hot topics like gun policy, are also concerned about so many other issues that they do not actively campaign for any of the possible issues under consideration. Despite what ideologues on either side would argue, the average American view on gun policy is that the United States should have BOTH gun rights AND gun control.[2]

The Future in Gun-Rights America

Donald Trump claimed, during his campaign, that he supported the controversial propositions that legal gun ownership and right-to-carry laws combined with mental-health screenings will reduce gun violence. His viewpoint combined with a Republican-controlled legislature, might well influence gun policy, at least in the near future. A number of well-founded, bipartisan academic studies have largely proven that mental-health is not a major factor in gun violence and while some incidents, like the Sandy Hook shooting, involve individuals with known mental health issues, the vast majority of gun crimes are not connected to mental illness.[3] Therefore, while gun rights advocates may continue to pursue this line of reasoning, there is no scientific or data-based evidence to support the proposal.

Nonetheless, it is clear that gun ownership is increasing. This provides an opportunity to study the hypothesis that concealed-carry licenses and armed civilians make the world safer. So far, a small number of studies in the 1990s supported the idea that right-to-carry reduces crime, but those studies have since fallen out of favor as newer, more comprehensive studies have found that right-to-carry and liberalizing gun ownership either has no effect on crime or leads to an increase in gun violence. As of 2017, the Centers for Disease Control and Prevention (CDC) and other funding organizations have been reluctant to study this issue due to Congressional threats to remove funding from the organization for allegedly supporting an anti-gun activist movement.[4]

Another characteristic conservative approach to gun policy involves enforcing current laws or creating stricter penalties for violations, rather than creating new laws. In the late 1990s, Tim Kaine (vice presidential candidate under Hillary Clinton) was one of the architects behind Richmond, Virginia's Project Exile, which essentially prosecuted gun offenders under federal, rather than state laws, and imposed mandatory, minimum sentences. As the program involved enforcing existing laws, rather than creating new ones, there was little resistance from gun-rights lobbyists.[5] After Project Exile, gun crimes plummeted in Richmond and the project has therefore met with bipartisan praise. Trump has since effectively appropriated the idea as the basis for possible future federal policy.

Project Exile seemed effective at reducing violence and gun crimes in Richmond, but, a lack of precise evaluation made the actual effects of the policy difficult to determine. At the same time that Exile was implemented, crime rates were already falling around the nation and no studies have yet proven that Project Exile led to a decline in crime beyond what the rest of the nation was experiencing without such laws in place. In addition, there are a number of serious criticisms of Project Exile, including the arguments that the program disproportionately targets African Americans and exacerbates the existing over-incarceration problem in the United States rather than providing services that might reduce the impetus and underlying causes of crime.

The Future in Gun-Control America

It is also possible that future legislative developments, legislative or presidential elections, or future high-profile incidents of gun violence may motivate a shift towards gun control. This will occur only if public opinion translates into voting behavior and so unseats some of the legislators who have been most strongly in support of the gun lobby's general "enact no new laws" position. The best data available suggests that reducing the availability of legal guns leads to a moderate reduction in gun violence, but these findings are based on an insufficient number of incomplete studies and there is a lack of data to constitute a proven cause-and-effect relationship.[6]

What would be more likely, in the case of a gun-control shift in America, would be that the legislature would pass laws that actually reflect the will of the majority of Americans. Current gun control policy, and the policies passed over the past 10 years, reflect the political ideology of a minority, composing perhaps 5 percent of the entire population, but these individuals vote based on gun policy and so carry far more weight than voters whose voting behavior is not tied to single-issue politics.[7] Even in this imagined future, there would be little realistic possibility that most Americans would want abolish the Second Amendment. While speakers at National Rifle Association (NRA) meetings and the propaganda and memes traded between gun-rights enthusiasts frequently assert that liberal politicians are going to "take away their Second Amendment freedoms," or similar alarmist sentiments, such a radical future is not a serious possibility in the near future.

Based on the best current information on public opinion, the future in a gun control-centric America would involve universal background checks for all gun sales, and would eliminate loopholes that allow individuals to get weapons without background checks in personal sales or through gun shows. In addition, if the majority had their way, ALL gun owners would be required to obtain a license before buying a gun. A Johns Hopkins Center study found that 70 percent of non-gun owners, and nearly 60 percent of gun owners supported this idea. Going by public opinion, Americans would also support prohibiting gun ownership for individuals convicted of domestic violence.[8] As of January 2017, a large majority of Americans support all of the above gun-control policies, but, because the majority does not make gun control one of their primary voting issues, legislators have remained respondent to the passionate minority who oppose such measures.

Time for Compromise?

One of the lessons from the 2016 political cycle was that misinformation, propaganda, and media manipulation can have a dramatic effect on public opinion. The proliferation of what has now been coined "fake news" is a major problem for media institutions struggling for legitimacy in the court of public opinion, especially as ideologues on both sides encourage their followers to reject legitimate news outlets as agents of an enemy ideological agenda.[9] It is in the public interest for all people, no matter their ideology, to take a more critical approach to the information they encounter, especially when delivered through social media or other potentially illegitimate sources.[10] There are organizations, like Snopes.com and FactCheck.org, that function solely to fact-check statements made by politicians, celebrities, circulated through the Internet or social media, or from a variety of other sources. These organizations are independent and nonpartisan and can help users to identify misinformation, outright lies, exaggerations, and other types of misleading information from individuals anywhere in the political spectrum.

Some gun-rights organizations, notably the NRA, have a history of downplaying information that might reduce popular support for gun ownership and promoting misleading information that might increase support for gun ownership. This bias demonstrates the problem with allowing organizations that are tied to commercial interests to play a major role in policy debates on key issues. The same skepticism might be levied at tobacco companies funding tobacco health concerns research or oil companies funding climate change research. Organizations like the CDC and the National Institutes of Health (NIH) are more appropriate sources for information because these organizations exist solely to identify and combat any and all health issues impacting the United States. The CDC and NIH promoted the dangers of tobacco despite resistance from the tobacco industry and, similarly, need to conduct research on gun violence and injuries, even if the information they uncover is potentially damaging to American business.[11] The failure to support scientific research on the subject weakens efforts to reach meaningful solutions on key issues and ultimately threatens the rights of the majority of Americans who occupy the middle ground on the gun-policy issue.

There is no legitimate reason that a gun-control advocate must necessarily favor abolishing the Second Amendment or believe that all gun owners are violent, or that a gun-rights supporter must necessarily believe that all guns should be legal or that stronger gun-control laws are akin to government tyranny. These extreme ideologies are the enemy of compromise, representing entrenched viewpoints typically based on emotion rather than reason and are generally paralyzing rather than productive.

Micah L. Issitt

Works Used:

Bialik, Carl. "In the Shadow of Exile." *FiveThirtyEight*. Five Thirty Eight. Jul 13 2016. Web. 28 Dec 2016.

Carroll, Lauren. "Obama: More Gun Laws Means Fewer Gun Deaths." *Politifact*. Politifact. Oct 6 2016. Web. 28 Dec 2016.

"Don't Get Spun by Internet Rumors." *Fact Check*. FactCheck.org. Dec 2016. Web. 1 Jan 2017.

Gold, Liza H. *Gun Violence and Mental Illness*. New York: American Psychiatric Publishing, Inc., 2015.

Hill, Steven and Robert Richie. "Why America Can't Pass Gun Control." *The Atlantic*. Atlantic Monthly Group. Dec 20 2012. Web. 28 Dec 2016.

Hiltzik, Michael. "The NRA Has Blocked Gun Violence Research for 20 Years. Let's End Its Stranglehold on Science." *Los Angeles Times*. Times Media. Jun 14 2016. Web. 1 Jan 2017.

Masters, Kate. "The CDC Just Released a 'Gun Violence' Study." *The Trace*. Dec 2 2015. Web. 28 Dec 2016.

McDonough, Katie. "Here's What US Gun Laws Would Look Like if a Majority of Americans Had Their Say." *Fusion*. Fusion Media Network, LLC. Aug 27 2015. Web. 29 Dec 2016.

Slattery, Denis. "Most Americans Want Stricter Gun Control, But Doubt It'll Happen." *New York Daily News*. Jul 23 2016. Web. 28 Dec 2016.

Vizzard, William J. "The Current and Future State of Gun Policy in the United States." *Journal of Criminal Law and Criminology*, Vol. 104, No. 4, Art. 5, Fall, 2015, 879-904.

Weinstein, Adam. "The NRA Was Waging War on Facts Long Before the 'Fake News' Boom." *The Trace*. Dec 12 2016. Web. 29 Dec 2016.

Notes

1. Hill and Richie, "Why America Can't Pass Gun Control."
2. Vizzard, "The Current and Future State of Gun Policy in the United States."
3. Gold, *Gun Violence and Mental Illness*.
4. Masters, "The CDC Just Released a 'Gun Violence' Study."
5. Bialik, "In the Shadow of Exile."
6. Carroll, "Obama: More Guns Laws Means Fewer Gun Deaths."
7. Slattery, "Most Americans Want Stricter Gun Control, But Doubt It'll Happen."
8. McDonough, "Here's What US Gun Laws Would Look Like if a Majority of Americans Had Their Say."
9. "Don't Get Spun by Internet Rumors," *Fact Check*.
10. Weinstein, "The NRA Was Waging War on Facts Long Before the 'Fake News' Boom."
11. Hiltzik, "The NRA has Blocked Gun Violence Research for 20 Years. Let's End It's Stranglehold on Science."

Donald Trump's Big Gun Idea? Literally Stolen from Tim Kaine

By Brandy Zadrozny
The Daily Beast, August 11, 2016

No one loves the Second Amendment more than Donald Trump, according to Donald Trump.

What's more, he says, only he can save it from the likes of Hillary Clinton, whom, he recently claimed without evidence in a seeming incitement of violence, would scrap the right to keep and bear arms from the Constitution.

As with most of his political opinions, the Republican presidential nominee's stance on gun rights has changed over the years. But Trump does have a plan to rescue the sacred yet apparently imperiled Second Amendment, one he lays out in his official position, published on his campaign website in September 2015.

Trump's plan calls for a number of policies, such as an expansion of gun rights and the overhaul of a "broken" mental health care system, common refrains from Second Amendment advocates. It begins, however, with another directive—"Enforce The Laws On The Books"—and as best practice, Trump invokes, but never names, Senator and Democratic vice presidential candidate Tim Kaine. Indeed, Trump's plan to Make America Great for Gun Owners Again leans heavily on Project Exile, a 1997 program Kaine implemented as mayor of Richmond, Virginia, that was aimed at driving down crime rates by elevating gun offenses to the tougher federal court system.

"Several years ago there was a tremendous program in Richmond, Virginia called Project Exile," Trump's policy reads.

"It said that if a violent felon uses a gun to commit a crime, you will be prosecuted in federal court and go to prison for five years—no parole or early release. Obama's former Attorney General, Eric Holder, called that a 'cookie cutter' program. That's ridiculous. I call that program a success. Murders committed with guns in Richmond decreased by over 60% when Project Exile was in place—in the first two years of the program alone, 350 armed felons were taken off the street."

It continues: "We need to bring back and expand programs like Project Exile and get gang members and drug dealers off the street. When we do, crime will go down and our cities and communities will be safer places to live."

Project Exile—implemented when the Richmond had the nation's third-highest murder rate per capita—was the result of a collaboration among federal prosecutors, law enforcement agents, local police, and state attorneys who agreed to prosecute qualifying gun crimes in federal court, where sentences were stiffer; bail, plea-bargains, and parole were unlikely; and, as the program's name suggests, time was usually served out of state, far from family and friends.

Word spread quickly. If a convicted felon was found carrying a gun during the commission of a crime, local prosecutors would now toss the case to the feds, who would seek sentences twice as harsh. The policy was blasted to would-be criminals in a massive advertising campaign. Billboards and city buses emblazoned with "An illegal gun gets you 5 years in Federal Prison," were funded in part by the NRA, which donated $125,000 to the marketing initiative.

"Our idea was, 'Let's do a lot of cases,' we'll incapacitate the worst gun carriers in Richmond and maybe will scare the rest of them through word of mouth into not carrying guns,'" then Deputy Assistant US Attorney James Comey said at the time.

"It's just amazing how afraid these guys are of the federal system," Kaine told *The Chicago Tribune* in 2000. "People who you think are tough and not afraid of anything, well, they're afraid of federal prison. So it means they think twice about taking their gun out with them."

The general consensus from politicians and law enforcement officials was that Project Exile worked. Cheerleaders for the program touted statistics showing an extreme reduction in crime: After one year, the homicide rate fell by over a third, and Assistant US Attorney David Schiller told the *New York Times* in 1999 that Project Exile had led to the recovery of 475 illegal guns, and more than 400 indictments.

Project Exile was so popular that even the NRA and the the Brady Campaign to Prevent Gun Violence, then known as Handgun Control, Inc., got behind the initiative, with NRA president Charlton Heston requesting $50 million at a House subcommittee hearing to expand Project Exile into more major cities. The bipartisan support for Project Exile was, as one committee member put it, "something that is unrivaled in the annals of history, perhaps only by Mr. Heston's parting of the Red Sea."

But not everyone was convinced.

Several federal judges labeled the practice as an overreach by the federal government into state matters, with one writing to Supreme Court Chief Justice William Rehnquist that Project Exile had turned his federal court into a "minor grade state police court."

"More than 200 gun possession cases totally lacking in Federal significance have been processed through our court," US District Judge Richard Williams wrote. Moreover, the cost of trying cases in federal court, which fell on taxpayers, was three times that of those tried at the state level, he said.

There was also a human cost, critics said. Local defense attorneys argued the program was inherently racist, prosecuting black city criminals almost exclusively under federal guidelines while their white suburban counterparts were tried in state courts. More recently, Black Lives Matter advocates have criticized Project Exile as a continuation of the 1990s initiatives enacted by former president Bill Clinton that led to the mass incarceration of the nation's black men and boys—policies from which Hillary Clinton has struggled to distance herself.

"Project Exile broke black families," Nicole Lee, a civil rights lawyer in Washington D.C., told Reuters last month. "This is not a benign thing to be for. These measures were not used against white kids in the suburbs with guns, they were used against black kids in the cities."

Perhaps the most damning critique of the initiative has come from academics who have questioned the reported success of what were, in effect, sentencing enhancements. An analysis from the University of Chicago found claims of Project Exile's accomplishments to be "misguided" and attributed the reduction of gun murders to other factors.

Despite its critics, Kaine has repeatedly offered the program as an example of his tough stance on crime and used Project Exile's overwhelming popularity to win elections. Kaine sat on Richmond's City Council when Project Exile was created in 1997. He was elected mayor in 1998. During his ultimately successful 2001 bid to be Virginia's lieutenant mayor, Kaine told *The Washington Post* that he had "[kept] our community safe from crime by implementing Project Exile."

> **The Republican nominee's plan to rescue the Second Amendment leans heavily on Project Exile, a program Hillary Clinton's running mate implemented as mayor of Richmond, Virginia.**

In 2003, then Lt. Governor Kaine criticized House Republicans who cut the program's funding. "As a leader in implementing Project Exile, I was able to see the positive impact this valuable and effective crime-fighting program had in Richmond and then statewide, and finally as a national model," Kaine wrote in a press release.

As a result, the program was slowly and unceremoniously phased out. Last week, an assistant Richmond commonwealth's attorney, told the *Richmond Times-Dispatch*, "I think officially Project Exile, as Project Exile, doesn't exist."

"As Mayor of Richmond, Tim Kaine helped implement 'Project Exile,'" his 2005 campaign website reads. Project Exile, it continues, "provide[s] a powerful illustration of the right way to combat the problem of gun violence: crack down on the criminals who use guns instead of restricting the rights of law-abiding gun owners."

Trump's campaign did not return a request for comment from *The Daily Beast*. But in numerous appearances and tweets since the announcement of Kaine as Clinton's running mate, Trump has attacked the pick as evidence of her questionable judgement.

"Tim Kaine—nobody even knows who he is. No, he's done a terrible job for Virginia," Trump said to supporters in Roanoke, Virginia, at a July rally.

One assumes he's not counting Kaine's "tremendous program in Richmond."

Print Citations

CMS: Zadrozny, Brandy. "Donald Trump's Big Gun Idea? Literally Stolen from Tim Kaine." In *The Reference Shelf: Guns in America*, edited by Betsy Maury, 155-57. Ipswich, MA: H.W. Wilson, 2017.

MLA: Zadrozny, Brandy. "Donald Trump's Big Gun Idea? Literally Stolen from Tim Kaine." *The Reference Shelf: Guns in America*. Ed. Betsy Maury. Ipswich: H.W. Wilson, 2017. 155-57. Print.

APA: Zadrozny, B. (2017). Donald Trump's big gun idea? Literally stolen from Tim Kaine. In Betsy Maury (Ed.), *The reference shelf: Guns in America* (pp. 155-57). Ipswich, MA: H.W. Wilson. (Original work published 2016)

Gun Control Advocates Find a Deep-Pocketed Ally in Big Law

By Jessica Silver-Greenberg and Ben Protess
The New York Times, December 7, 2016

In Congress and in the Supreme Court, the gun lobby has racked up some crucial victories in recent years. It won again last month when Donald J. Trump, buoyed by the lobby's money and support, secured an upset victory in the presidential election.

On the defensive, gun control advocates are now quietly developing a plan to chip away at the gun lobby's growing clout: Team up with corporate law firms.

After the Orlando nightclub massacre and a string of other mass shootings, Paul, Weiss, Rifkind, Wharton & Garrison; Covington & Burling; Arnold & Porter; and four other prominent law firms formed a coalition with gun control groups that until now have worked largely on their own. Together, the firms are committing tens of millions of dollars in free legal services from top corporate lawyers who typically bill clients $1,000 an hour or more.

This effort is highly unusual in its scale. Although law firms often donate time to individual causes, and some firms have worked on gun control on a piecemeal basis, the number and the prominence of the firms involved in the new coalition are unheard-of for modern-day big law. Other firms are expected to join in the coming months.

It is also the first time in decades that rival corporate law firms, more accustomed to beating back regulation than championing it, have joined forces to file litigation nationwide around such a polarizing social issue as guns. The effort harks back to the civil rights era, when President John F. Kennedy summoned 250 top lawyers to the White House and enlisted their help in fighting segregation.

Just as significant, the gun coalition plans to pursue new legal strategies to avoid some previous pitfalls.

Rather than fighting the political headwinds, the coalition is focusing on courts and state regulatory agencies, among the few places where they might still gain some traction. The coalition is drafting lawsuits and preparing regulatory complaints that could be announced as soon as next month, according to the Law Center to Prevent Gun Violence, one of the nonprofit advocacy groups that helped form the coalition, along with the Brady Center to Prevent Gun Violence and the Brennan Center for Justice, a legal think tank at New York University School of Law.

On one front, the coalition will seek to overturn state laws that have gone largely unchallenged, including new policies that force businesses to allow guns to be carried on their property. The group also plans to mount the first formal challenges to congressional restrictions on publishing government data on gun violence. Taking a page from the fight against big tobacco two decades ago, it will seek the help of regulators to challenge what it views as the gun industry's attempts to stifle competition.

"This coalition brings together more resources, more brainpower and more lawyers dedicated to making our clients and our nation safer," said Charlie Lifland, the O'Melveny & Myers partner leading the firm's work with the coalition.

But the law firms—which also include Dentons; Munger, Tolles & Olson; and Hogan Lovells—could run into fierce opposition.

Mr. Trump, a Republican, has vowed to defend the Second Amendment and expand protections for gun owners. And by taking on a third-rail political issue like gun control, the firms, which typically defend Wall Street and even big tobacco, could develop some tension with the Trump administration and encounter resistance from their own roster of clients aligned with the gun industry.

The National Rifle Association will also continue to have considerable advantages—political and organizational—over the coalition and other groups seeking to curb gun violence.

"The power of the NRA lies with our members and the tens of millions of Americans who support the Second Amendment," said Jennifer Baker, a spokeswoman for the organization's lobbying arm. "The gun control lobby made this election a referendum on gun control, and they lost because the majority of Americans support the Second Amendment and they vote to protect their constitutional right to self-protection."

In statements to *The New York Times*, some of the firms emphasized that their effort was aimed not at eroding gun rights but at preventing gun violence.

"Those of us working on this effort recognize that the Second Amendment is an important part of our Constitution, and we don't take issue with responsible gun owners," said Brad D. Brian, co-managing partner at Munger, Tolles & Olson. But he added, "There is an epidemic of gun violence in this country, and the law can save innocent lives without infringing constitutional rights."

Richard M. Alexander, the chairman of Arnold & Porter, called the coalition an effective way of "addressing the worsening scourge of gun violence that plagues this country."

Brad S. Karp, the chairman of Paul, Weiss, first alluded to the coalition in an email to colleagues just hours after the Orlando nightclub tragedy: "It is in our DNA to act when we see injustice," referring to the firm's work on same-sex marriage.

But gun control is a thornier political issue than those that law firms typically mobilize around, and until now, there has not been a coordinated effort across the firms to mount a broad offensive.

"With this new coalition, our bench just got deeper," said Avery Gardiner, the Brady Center's chief legal officer.

For years, corporate law partners at Skadden Arps, Ropes & Gray, Mayer Brown and other prominent firms have donated time to the Brady Center or individual gun control cases. Covington and O'Melveny & Myers represented the District of Columbia in a landmark Supreme Court case, *D.C. v. Heller*, which overturned a ban on handguns.

The Brady Center has also tapped private law firms to assist in suing gun dealers and manufacturers. Some of these efforts have been successful, including when the Brady Center won a $5 million verdict against a Milwaukee gun seller last year, but the 2005 federal law known as the Protection of Lawful Commerce in Arms Act largely shields gun manufacturers and dealers from legal liability.

The creation of the coalition, which the groups named the Firearms Accountability Counsel Task Force, amounts to a tacit acknowledgment that the federal shield law has undercut the approach to litigating against the gun industry. In the most recent development, a federal judge in Connecticut dismissed a lawsuit that the relatives of victims in the attack at Sandy Hook Elementary School brought against an assault rifle manufacturer.

> **Although law firms often donate time to individual causes, and some firms have worked on gun control on a piecemeal basis, the number and the prominence of the firms involved in the new coalition are unheard-of for modern-day big law.**

The coalition of law firms and nonprofit organizations will continue to work around the edges of that law—challenging the relatively small number of gun dealers who account for most firearms used in crimes—but its strategy hinges on new lines of attack. Eric M. Ruben, a fellow at the Brennan Center for Justice, which, unlike the gun control advocacy groups, is a legal research institute, spent more than a year looking for new legal strategies.

One fresh avenue of litigation would involve challenging state laws that arguably force citizens and local governments to allow guns to be carried on their properties, including schools, airports, shopping malls and bars. Such laws, the coalition argues, could infringe on property rights and threaten the safety of customers and employees.

Separately, the coalition is considering taking aim at Congress's longtime restriction on the Bureau of Alcohol, Tobacco, Firearms and Explosives from releasing certain data about the use of firearms in crimes. The coalition might also challenge a congressional policy that effectively chokes off funding to government research on the potential public health threat of guns.

"We took a step back and thought about creative ways we could bring to light what the industry is doing," said Robyn Thomas, the executive director of the Law Center to Prevent Gun Violence, who helped organize the coalition, along with her litigation director, Adam Skaggs. (The law center is the legal arm of the gun safety organization founded by Gabrielle Giffords, a former Democratic congresswoman from Arizona, and her husband.)

The coalition is also examining lawsuits against the gun industry over possible antitrust violations. In the past, some gun companies joined forces, the coalition said, to curb efforts by competitors to develop safety technology, including firearms that will not go off unless held by their registered owners.

Another prominent advocacy group, Everytown for Gun Safety—backed in part by Michael R. Bloomberg, a political independent who was New York's mayor—did not join the coalition. But the Everytown group, which will continue to focus on pushing for gun safety legislation and defending those laws in court, said the new coalition was an "encouraging moment" in the fight against gun violence.

The coalition hopes state regulators and prosecutors might join one or several of these cases.

The Manhattan district attorney, Cyrus R. Vance Jr., a Democrat, is one potential partner. While receiving an award from the Law Center to Prevent Gun Violence last year, Mr. Vance and Ms. Thomas discussed the possibility of a coalition with law firms.

He offered to arrange a meeting with some of the top lawyers in New York. And so, last March, lawyers from about a dozen firms, including Marc E. Kasowitz of Kasowitz, Benson, Torres & Friedman, joined Ms. Thomas for lunch in Mr. Vance's office.

Afterward, several of the firms pledged to help. But Mr. Kasowitz, who has represented Mr. Trump, said recently that although Mr. Vance had done some admirable work on gun issues, his firm was not part of the new coalition.

Print Citations

CMS: Silver-Greenberg, Jessica, and Ben Protess. "Gun Control Advocates Find a Deep-Pocketed Ally in Big Law." In *The Reference Shelf: Guns in America*, edited by Betsy Maury, 159-62. Ipswich, MA: H.W. Wilson, 2017.

MLA: Silver-Greenberg, Jessica, and Ben Protess. "Gun Control Advocates Find a Deep-Pocketed Ally in Big Law." *The Reference Shelf: Guns in America*. Ed. Betsy Maury. Ipswich: H.W. Wilson, 2017. 159-62. Print.

APA: Silver-Greenberg, J., & B. Protess. (2017). Gun control advocates find a deep-pocketed ally in big law. In Betsy Maury (Ed.), *The reference shelf: Guns in America* (pp. 159-62). Ipswich, MA: H.W. Wilson. (Original work published 2016)

Under Donald Trump, What Will Happen on Guns?

By Michele Gorman
Newsweek, **November 17, 2016**

Throughout his almost 17-month presidential campaign, Donald Trump vowed that, if elected, he would "totally" protect the Second Amendment. He even has promised to swiftly "unsign" the executive actions President Barack Obama issued in January to streamline the gun purchase background checks system and to abolish gun-free zones at schools and on military bases, which he called "a catastrophe." He also said he wanted to implement national right to carry in all 50 states, and he appeared to suggest that gun rights advocates should take lethal action against his Democratic rival, Hillary Clinton, should she be elected president and threaten the Second Amendment by appointing a far-left justice to the US Supreme Court. (His campaign later said he was referring to convincing supporters of the Second Amendment to rally votes for him.) And, just five days before the presidential election, he formed a 64-member Second Amendment coalition—featuring National Rifle Association board members, pro-gun US representatives and firearms manufacturers—that seeks to advise him on protecting the constitutional right to keep and bear arms.

Now that he has won the election, what will President-elect Trump actually do when it comes to gun laws? During the campaign, the billionaire businessman touted many big plans—including building a wall at the Mexican border, changing US trade relations and backing away from climate change agreements—but in the week since his victory he has appeared to soften his tone on some of his key complaints, including saying he wants to repeal *only parts* of Obamacare and contemplating not prosecuting Clinton for her use of a private email account as secretary of state.

On the guns issue, one prominent Democrat says she is optimistic Trump will live up to his promise to shake up Washington and not be beholden to the political party he represents. "In the Nixon goes to China mode, Donald Trump may be exactly the president who could do something positive on gun safety," US Representative Elizabeth Esty of Connecticut tells *Newsweek*. Esty, who represents the district where the 2012 Sandy Hook Elementary School mass shooting took place, is vice chairwoman of the House Gun Violence Prevention Task Force.

Gun rights were a potent issue in the 2016 campaign. Trump planted himself firmly on the side of gun owners with his "law-and-order" campaign and channeled some of the NRA's most incendiary rhetoric. He said he's in favor of empowering gun owners to defend themselves and thwart crime, has called on the government to expand gun rights for law-abiding Americans and has argued that arming civilians could stop mass killings. He said he opposes new gun-control measures and even owns and carries a gun in his home state of New York, "sometimes a lot."

The campaign named Chris Cox, the NRA's executive director, and one of Trump's sons, Donald Jr.—an avid hunter and outspoken proponent of gun rights—as the chairmen to lead his Second Amendment coalition. Antonio Hernández Almodóvar, who is part of the group and an attorney in San Juan, Puerto Rico, says it's unclear when the members will meet or start to advise Trump. In the meantime, he says his two goals for the administration are to prosecute criminals who try to purchase guns—instead of placing restrictions on lawful gun owners—and to institute National Right-to-Carry Reciprocity legislation. "I think it's fair that if we have a good citizen who's law-abiding in one state, that he does not fear prosecution because he crosses state lines or he goes to another state to enjoy the sport," he tells *Newsweek*.

The NRA might push ahead most aggressively on the reciprocity bill, says Robert Spitzer, Political Science Department chairman at the State University of New York at Cortland. The measure would force states that allow concealed carry to recognize each other's permits, similar to driver's licenses. Opponents argue that would enable the least restrictive requirements to apply to the whole country, thus undercutting stricter requirements in some states. But such legislation in the past has been backed by members in both chambers of Congress and could soon land on Trump's desk in the Oval Office. Just this week, the NRA's executive vice president and chief executive officer, Wayne LaPierre, in a video message requested that Trump enact such reciprocity legislation "as quickly as it can be written and signed." He also asked Trump and lawmakers to abolish gun-free zones and get rid of bans on certain firearms, types of ammunition and large-capacity magazines. An NRA spokesperson didn't respond to *Newsweek*'s requests for additional information on the organization's goals under Trump's administration.

Another member of the Second Amendment coalition, US Representative Tom Emmer of Minnesota, says he looks forward to working with Trump to roll back Obama's "overreaching, executive actions" on guns. "Under President Obama, Americans witnessed numerous unilateral actions seeking to deprive law-abiding Americans of their Second Amendment rights. Thankfully, we now have the opportunity to reverse course," he tells *Newsweek* in an email. Specifically, Emmer wants to work with Trump to pass the Firearm Due Process Protection Act, legislation he introduced in April that seeks to ensure Americans can correct false information if they are denied owning a gun.

Before the election, both Trump and the NRA told Americans that the future of the US Supreme Court rested on their votes. The president-elect has promised to appoint a pro-Second Amendment justice to fill the seat left vacant when conservative Justice Antonin Scalia died suddenly in February. But that nomination likely would simply restore the Scalia-era balance to the court. It was Scalia who wrote the landmark *District of Columbia v. Heller* ruling eight years ago, when the court recognized an individual right to keep guns at home for self-defense. Since then, though, the justices have declined to review dozens of cases that have upheld gun-related bans. It likely would take another Supreme Court appointment to shift the balance on the issue. Trump has made it clear how he views it: "Gun and magazine bans," he said in his position paper, "are a total failure."

But Trump wasn't always such a strong supporter of gun ownership. Before he became a presidential candidate, the businessman called out Republicans who "walk the NRA line" and "refuse even limited restrictions" on firearms laws. "I generally oppose gun control, but I support the ban on assault weapons and I also support a slightly longer waiting period to purchase a gun," he wrote in his 2000 book, *The America We Deserve*. At the time, he was considering a bid for the presidency but hadn't declared his intention to run.

Fourteen years later, in April 2014, Trump made an appearance at a pro-gun rally in Albany, New York, and spoke about the importance of protecting the Second Amendment. The next year—two months before he entered the presidential race—he told those gathered at an NRA forum: "I love the NRA. I love the Second Amendment." He went further during a debate this year in March, saying he no longer supported a ban on assault weapons. In May, the NRA endorsed him, and it then spent heavily to bolster his campaign. The group was one of the few enthusiastic organized backers of Trump, as most other conservative groups sidestepped the former reality TV star's campaign.

> But Trump wasn't always such a strong supporter of gun ownership. Before he became a presidential candidate, the businessman called out Republicans who "walk the NRA line" and "refuse even limited restrictions" on firearms laws.

In general, the debate over the need for gun control could become more muted with the GOP controlling both houses of Congress and a Republican in the White House, and with Democratic lawmakers in red states—including senators Joe Manchin of West Virginia and Heidi Heitkamp of North Dakota—up for re-election in 2018 and thus unlikely to be as outspoken on the issue.

One wild card, however, is the idea put forth by Spitzer and others that Trump simply used his guns stance to establish his conservative credentials on the campaign trail, and that loosening gun restrictions is not really a top-tier issue for him. In the wake of the deadliest mass shooting in US history—in June at the Pulse nightclub in Orlando, Florida—Trump appeared to show support for prohibiting known or suspected terrorists from buying guns. Those who oppose stricter gun laws, including many in the Republican Party, have stood firm against such a change. The NRA has said it wants to ensure that Americans wrongly placed on the no-fly list are given their legal rights to due process.

Regardless of what happens at the federal level during Trump's presidency, gun-control groups including Everytown for Gun Safety are promising to build on their momentum in the fight for stricter legislation at the state level. On Election Day, measures seeking to tighten gun laws passed in three out of four states where they were on the ballot. While Everytown endorsed Clinton in the presidential race, says the group's chief communications officer, Erika Soto Lamb, it doesn't view her loss as "a statement about gun safety in America."

Print Citations

CMS: Gorman, Michele. "Under Donald Trump, What Will Happen on Guns?" In *The Reference Shelf: Guns in America*, edited by Betsy Maury, 163-66. Ipswich, MA: H.W. Wilson, 2017.

MLA: Gorman, Michele. "Under Donald Trump, What Will Happen on Guns?" *The Reference Shelf: Guns in America*. Ed. Betsy Maury. Ipswich: H.W. Wilson, 2017. 163-66. Print.

APA: Gorman, M. (2017). Under Donald Trump, what will happen on guns? In Betsy Maury (Ed.), *The reference shelf: Guns in America* (pp. 163-66). Ipswich, MA: H.W. Wilson. (Original work published 2016)

Gun Laws and Terrorism: An American Nightmare

By John Cassidy
The New Yorker, June 13, 2016

On Sunday, around lunchtime, I took my two daughters and our puppy to a dog park in Brooklyn Heights, near the East River. It was a fine, breezy day, and throngs of people were strolling along the raised promenade, which provides a view of New York Harbor and downtown Manhattan. With Americans of all colors and creeds enjoying the sunshine, I felt like I was in an urban version of a Norman Rockwell painting.

Except, that is, for the iPhone in my pocket, which was providing updates from the attack at a gay night club in Orlando the night before: Twenty dead. Thirty dead. Fifty dead. Fifty-three wounded. Suspect named Omar Mateen, a twenty-nine-year-old American citizen of Afghan descent. The suspect's former wife says that he beat her and wasn't particularly religious. The suspect called 911 shortly before carrying out the massacre and pledged allegiance to ISIS. The suspect had been investigated by the FBI, twice. The suspect had legally purchased a pistol and an assault rifle a few days prior to the attack.

Looking at the stream of bulletins, it was hard to do anything but weep for the victims, their families, and the future of this country. But the fight soon began over who was to blame and what should be done.

The history isn't really in dispute. It has been clear for years that the combination of America's ludicrously lax gun laws and calls from Al Qaeda and ISIS for individuals, or groups, in Western countries to carry out terrorist attacks could produce horrific outcomes. For a time, the United States largely escaped such attacks, which have hit London, Paris, and many cities in the Middle East and Africa. But the country's bizarre adherence to an expansive reading of the Second Amendment—a reading that the Supreme Court Justice Warren Burger described, in 1990, as a "fraud on the American public"—has left it acutely vulnerable to attacks by radicalized or disturbed individuals.

The shooting spree at Fort Hood, in 2009, which killed thirteen people, and the April, 2013, Boston Marathon bombings, which killed three people, hinted at what lay ahead. For whatever reason, the Tsarnaev brothers, at least one of whom appears to have advocated jihad, selected homemade explosives as their weapon of choice. But the seemingly endless series of mass shootings at schools, cinemas, churches, places of work, and other locations in the United States has shown us how deadly assault weapons can be. All that a US citizen who wants to kill a lot of people has to do is drive to a local gun store, ask to purchase a couple of AR-15 rifles and some ammunition, pass a background check, get the weapons, and select a site. It is easier than hijacking a plane or assembling a truck bomb.

We have seen the pattern with guns play out repeatedly—three times in the past year with shooters who appear to have been influenced by ISIS or Al Qaeda, the casualty toll rising each time. Last July, Muhammad Youssef Abdulazeez, a Kuwaiti-born American citizen, opened fire on two military installations in Chattanooga, Tennessee, killing five people and wounding another two. A subsequent investigation found that he had a history of mental problems, and that he had legally purchased at least some of the guns he used, which included two assault rifles.

On December 2nd of last year, Syed Rizwan Farook and Tashfeen Malik, a married couple whom James Comey, the director of the FBI, subsequently described as "homegrown violent extremists," opened fire at a government building in San Bernardino, California, killing fourteen people and seriously wounding twenty-two. It turned out that they had

> But the country's bizarre adherence to an expansive reading of the Second Amendment—a reading that the Supreme Court Justice Warren Burger described, in 1990, as a "fraud on the American public"— has left it acutely vulnerable to attacks by radicalized or disturbed individuals.

stockpiled a small armory, including two .223-calibre assault rifles, two semi-automatic handguns, and thousands of rounds of ammunition. They had purchased the handguns themselves, at a gun store called Annie's Get Your Gun, while a neighbor had purchased the two rifles for them.

Four days after the San Bernardino shootings, President Obama delivered a prime-time address from the Oval Office, in which he said that Farook and Malik "had gone down the dark path of radicalization, embracing a perverted interpretation of Islam that calls for war against America and the West." Obama called on Congress to "make sure no one on a no-fly list is able to buy a gun," and added, "What could possibly be the argument for allowing a terrorist suspect to buy a semi-automatic weapon? This is a matter of national security."

The Republican-controlled Congress ignored these words, just as it had frustrated the Obama Administration's efforts to strengthen gun laws after the Sandy Hook massacre, which took place in December, 2012. "Sandy Hook marked the end of the US gun control debate," Dan Hodges, a British journalist, tweeted in June of last year. "Once America decided killing children was bearable, it was over."

If Hodges was right and the United States will never take action on gun control, then it is heading toward a future where much of the country is a fortified camp, with stricter rules governing who is allowed in, heavily armed police permanently patrolling urban hubs, more public buildings adopting airport-style security, and many more millions of guns sold, as alarmed citizens seek to protect themselves and their families against a perceived threat.

This is the low-trust equilibrium that Donald Trump and other supporters of "gun rights" appear to favor. Alternatively, the United States could respond to the deadliest mass shooting in its history by shaking off the straitjacket of the past, disproving the skeptics, and reforming laws that have proved to be a boon to those intent on doing harm. In this scenario, guns (particularly assault weapons) would be much harder to come by; borders would be secure, but not impermeable; heavy security would be focused on vulnerable locations, rather than everywhere; and the burden of preventing terrorism and other violent attacks would fall on the police, the intelligence agencies, and a vigilant public.

In either of these versions of the United States, sadly, there would probably be more terrorist attacks, some of them carried out by US citizens and inspired from abroad: nobody can disinvent ISIS, Al Qaeda, or the deadly sectarianism that these groups represent. Even if ISIS were to be soundly defeated in Iraq and Syria, diminishing its attractiveness to the young and impressionable, there would still be some people who sought to kill in its name. But the two versions of the United States would feel very different to live in: one would be more like other advanced countries; the other would be a nightmare.

Hopefully, the choice is still ours to make.

Print Citations

CMS: Cassidy, John. "Gun Laws and Terrorism: An American Nightmare." In *The Reference Shelf: Guns in America*, edited by Betsy Maury, 167-69. Ipswich, MA: H.W. Wilson, 2017.

MLA: Cassidy, John. "Gun Laws and Terrorism: An American Nightmare." *The Reference Shelf: Guns in America*. Ed. Betsy Maury. Ipswich: H.W. Wilson, 2017. 167-69. Print.

APA: Cassidy, J. (2017). Gun laws and terrorism: An American nightmare. In Betsy Maury (Ed.), *The reference shelf: Guns in America* (pp. 167-69). Ipswich, MA: H.W. Wilson. (Original work published 2016)

Quantifying the Social Cost of Firearms: A New Approach to Gun Control

By Timothy M. Smith

The Conversation, July 12, 2016

Another week in America, another week of sadness and hand-wringing prompted by gun violence.

While the most recent incidents are tinged by race, they also point to a country awash in guns and the too many deaths that result from their use (or abuse). But are these shootings any more likely to lead to some kind of meaningful action to address the problem?

Unfortunately, probably not. As long as the debate continues to be one of constitutionality (the right to bear arms) and control (regulation), little meaningful change is likely to address the 16 million new guns entering the US market each year or the nearly 34,000 annual gun deaths.

A new dialogue is desperately needed among policymakers and the public. And it could begin by shifting our focus away from the regulation of guns toward understanding (and mitigating) the social costs of firearm fatalities.

My research examines ways to assess the social, environmental and health effects of new technologies to inform policymakers and companies. Though my focus at the University of Minnesota is on sustainability, similar analyses may also be useful for the political debate over gun control.

Firearm Fatalities

The current congressional debate focuses on the most violent actors (terrorists or those whose background check may not check out) and the most lethal guns (military-style rifles)—not necessarily the deadliest guns or those creating the greatest risks to society.

Despite the headlines, most guns never kill anyone, and military-style rifles are some of the least frequently used guns in firearm deaths. Each year, fewer than one firearm-related death occurs in the US for every 10,000 guns in circulation, or 33,636 fatalities for an estimated 357 million guns. And about two-thirds of those deaths are suicides.

Gun deaths associated with mass shootings have surged dramatically in recent years, but are still rare compared with other gun violence. In just the first four months of 2016, 70 mass shootings have been reported (more than all of 2015), with 129 victim fatalities, according to Stanford University's Mass Shootings in America. Adding in Orlando and Dallas, mass shooting deaths in the first half of 2016 equal those of 2015 and are four times the annual average in recent years.

While this is alarming, such deaths represent just a fraction of the number of firearm-related homicides, about 1.6 percent. And military-style rifles were used in just 10 of the 136 mass shootings reported since January 2015.

Any policy to reduce the likelihood of these events should, therefore, reflect the very small probability of a military-style rifle being used in a mass shooting that targets the public—just one in 575,000 (about 50 deaths out of about 29 million rifles).

New regulation would need to be very restrictive. Millions of these guns would have to be removed from circulation to see any measurable effect on public safety, a politically impossible lift.

Price Tag of Saving a Life

A potential reframing of the issue might be to estimate the social cost of gun deaths, establish the burden borne by each weapon and seek policies that reflect it in the market for firearms.

Across many different areas of government, this kind of analysis is applied all the time when examining the benefits and costs of potential policies. When considering food handling or tracking systems, benefits of reducing the risk of illness and premature death are compared with the costs of implementing the policy. Policies to reduce harmful pollution, improve the safety of automobiles or add bicycle lanes to roads are evaluated in similar ways.

To get at a social cost of mortality, measures have been developed to assess how much people are willing to pay for small reductions in their risks of dying. In aggregate, these values are referred to as the "value of a statistical life" (VSL).

This is not how much an actual individual life is worth, but it is an estimate of how much, in total, a large group of people would be willing to pay to save one statistical life. For example, if the average response from a sample of 100,000 people indicated a willingness to pay US$100 to reduce their risk of dying by 0.001 percent, than the VSL would be $10,000,000. So, the total economic cost of mortality in a particular year equals the VSL times the number of premature deaths. Similarly, the economic benefit of a mitigating action becomes the same VSL multiplied by the number of lives saved.

That said, different federal agencies use various valuation methods and assumption. The Environmental Protection Agency's adjusted VSL for 2013 is $9.4 million, the Department of Transportation set its 2013 base year value at $9.1 million and the Department of Agriculture provides a midpoint estimate of $8.66 million.

From a purely economic perspective, the social costs of gun deaths likely exceed $300 billion annually. This is a staggering number, more than what the federal government spent on Medicaid in the same year. And that's not including the more than 80,000 nonfatal firearm injuries each year.

A Gun's Burden

Identifying guns' overall mortality risk burden doesn't exactly help inform legislation targeting certain types of guns used in certain types of homicides.

But, based on the previous analysis of military-style rifles used in mass shootings, these guns (in these situations) are some of the least costly from a VSL perspective. In fact, the social burden of a single military-style rifle is likely to be as little as $15.77 a year (or $455 million for all rifles based on 50 deaths and a $9.1 million VSL).

It is hard to see how this valuation could deter gun sales enough, or support the implementation of a robust screening and background check system, to make a difference. By comparison, handguns—which are implicated in nearly 70 percent of gun-related homicides—bear a disproportionate burden on society of $401 annually per handgun in circulation.

Policies reducing the burden of gun deaths (e.g., by reducing the number of guns or improving their safety) need to be compared against the additional costs of implementing them. These costs could come as regulations, increased taxes/fees or price increases.

In other words, applying a mortality risk valuation to handguns might cost as much every year as the initial cost to the gun owner. In the current climate, any form of tax or fee approaching this valuation would be a political nonstarter.

A Way Forward

So, if this analysis leads to societal burdens that are both so low (the case of rifles) and so high (the case of handguns) that neither are politically viable, one can easily understand the paralysis in Congress.

The automobile insurance market, where risks are pooled across geographies, types of vehicles and driving behavior, may provide some insights and a way forward.

Similar to guns, nearly 250 million personal vehicles (or their drivers) were associated with 27,507 deaths in 2013. These premature fatalities tally social costs of $250 billion.

For illustrative purposes, if we assume that half of these damages are associated with no-fault third parties, the social burden for non-policy-holder deaths might be about $502 per vehicle, on average.

Unlike with guns, a robust system of vehicle registration and mandatory insurance requirements exists in this market. If we also assume that about half of each auto's liability policy (estimated at $519 in 2013) covers bodily injuries (not property), these insurance premiums represent about half of each vehicle's societal burden.

I'm not suggesting that these premiums are effective deterrents to poor driving or cover all an accident's damages to society. Rather, incorporating the external costs of mortality risks into the cost of ownership alters the number of cars on the road and how they are used.

Applying this relationship to firearms, an annual social price tag of $140 per gun might go a long way toward mitigating the mortality costs of gun-related homicide. This estimate is a weighted average of different types of guns, ranging from $15/year for rifles to $200/year for handguns.

Nobody likes new taxes or additional fees, and the gun lobby will certainly oppose even the hint of a disincentive on gun ownership. But there may be enough Republican and Democrat lawmakers open to the idea of market-based policies that don't directly restrict gun access, progressively impose higher costs to more dangerous guns and generate resources to improve the safety and security associated with guns in America.

Gun Reform Doesn't Have to Be Gun Control

This back-of-the-napkin analysis may be crude, but it does highlight the need and potential for shifting current arguments away from regulating guns to mitigating the social costs of gun-related deaths.

The devil is always in the details, and important debates will be needed around the imposition of new taxes, registration fees or mandatory insurance. It is unclear who should be affected (owners, retailers, manufacturers) or how to include all of the estimated 357 million guns in the U.S., not just the registered ones.

Policymakers should even consider the impact of these types of economic mechanisms on equity of gun ownership—maybe gun subsidies would be needed for low-income or first-time gun buyers. Most importantly, policymakers should have much-needed arguments about how to reduce gun deaths.

An $140 annual registration fee, applied only to the 23.1 million guns transacted each year, could generate over $3.2 billion in revenues annually. If nothing else, these resources could bolster local police and security budgets, improve access to gun safety training and education, incentivize new technologies that make guns less dangerous and compensate victims' families.

Anything to break the logjam and actually address the real costs of gun violence.

Print Citations

CMS: Smith, Timothy M. "Quantifying the Social Cost of Firearms: A New Approach to Gun Control." In *The Reference Shelf: Guns in America*, edited by Betsy Maury, 170-73. Ipswich, MA: H.W. Wilson, 2017.

MLA: Smith, Timothy M. "Quantifying the Social Cost of Firearms: A New Approach to Gun Control." *The Reference Shelf: Guns in America*. Ed. Betsy Maury. Ipswich: H.W. Wilson, 2017. 170-73. Print.

APA: Smith, T.M. (2017). Quantifying the social cost of firearms: A new approach to gun control. In Betsy Maury (Ed.), *The reference shelf: Guns in America* (pp. 170-73). Ipswich, MA: H.W. Wilson. (Original work published 2016)

Bibliography

"2016 Global Peace Index." *Vision of Humanity*. Institute for Economics and Peace. IEP Report 39. June 2016. Pdf. 28 Dec 2016.

Acosta, Luis. "United States: Gun Ownership and the Supreme Court." *LOC*. Library of Congress. July 2008. Web. 25 Dec 2016.

Barnes, Robert. "Supreme Court Won't Review Laws Banning Assault Weapons." *The Washington Post*. Nash Holdings. Dec 7 2015. Web. 26 Dec 2016.

Beckett, Lois. "The Assault Weapon Myth." *New York Times*. New York Times Company. Sep 12 2014. Web. 27 Dec 2016.

Bellesiles, Michael A. *Arming America: The Origins of a National Gun Culture*. New York: Alfred A. Knopf, 2000.

Bialik, Carl. "In the Shadow of Exile." *FiveThirtyEight*. Five Thirty Eight. Jul 13 2016. Web. 28 Dec 2016.

———. "Most Americans Agree with Obama That More Gun Buyers Should Get Background Checks." *FiveThirtyEight*. Five Thirty Eight. Jan 5 2016. Web. 27 Dec 2016.

Blake, John. "Does Race Shape Americans' Passion for Guns?" *CNN*. Cable News Network. Oct 12 2014. Web. 28 Dec 2016.

Brabner-Smith, John. "Firearm Regulation." Law and Contemporary Problems. Vol. 1, No. 4, 1934, 400–14. Pdf. 25 Dec 2016.

Brennan, Allison. "Analysis: Fewer US Gun Owners Own More Guns." *CNN Politics*. Jul 31 2012. Web. 28 Dec 2016.

Carroll, Lauren. "Obama: More Gun Laws Means Fewer Gun Deaths." *Politifact*. Politifact. Oct 6 2016. Web. 28 Dec 2016.

Cassidy, John. "The Saliency Bias and 9/11: Is America Recovering?" *The New Yorker*. Condé Nast. Sep 11 2013. Web. 26 Dec 2016.

Chapman, Simon, Alpers, Philip, and Michael Jones. "Association Between Gun Law Reforms and Intentional Firearm Deaths in Australia, 1979–2013." Journal of the American Medical Association, Vol. 316, No. 3, July 19, 2016, 291-99.

Childress, Sarah and Chris Amico. "How Loaded Is the Gun Lobby?" *PBS Frontline*. Public Broadcasting Service. Jan 6 2015. Web. 25 Dec 2016.

"Concealed Carry Permit Holders Across the United States." *CPRC*. Crime Prevention Research Center. Jul 9 2014. Web. 27 Dec 2016.

"Crime in the United States 2014." *FBI*. Federal Bureau of Investigation. Criminal Justice Information Services Division. 2014. Pdf. 28 Dec 2016.

Coulter, Ann. "Guns Don't Kill People, the Mentally Ill Do." *Ann Coulter*. Ann Coulter. Jan 16 2013. Web. 29 Dec 2016.

Davis, Sean. "The Assault Weapons Ban Is a Stupid Idea Pushed by Stupid People." *The Federalist*. FDRLST Media. Jun 13 2016. Web. 26 Dec 2016.

DeBrabander, Firmin. *Do Guns Make Us Free?: Democracy and the Armed Society*. New Haven, CT: Yale University Press, 2015.

"Don't Get Spun by Internet Rumors." *Fact Check*. FactCheck.org. Dec 2016. Web. 1 Jan 2017.

"Editorial: What to Do about Assault Weapons." *Chicago Tribune*. Jun 14 2016. Web. 26 Dec 2016.

"Firearms and Violence: A Critical Review." *NAP*. National Academices of Science. Naitonal Research Council. 2004. Pdf. 29 Dec 2016.

Flatley, John. "Crime in England and Wales: Year Ending March 2015." *ONS*. Office for National Statistics. Jul 16 2015. Web. 28 Dec 2016.

Flowers, Andrew. "The Problem with Using the Terrorist Watch List To Ban Gun Sales." *Five Thirty Eight*. Five Thirty Eight. Jun 20 2016. Web. 27 Dec 2016.

Foran, Clare. "The Missing Data on Gun Violence." *Atlantic*. Atlantic Monthly Group. Jan 21 2016. Web. 26 Dec 2016.

Ford, Matt. "What Caused the Great Crime Decline in the U.S.?" *Atlantic*. Atlantic Monthly Group. Apr 15 2016. Web. 26 Dec 2016.

Fortunado, David. "Can Easing Concealed Carry Deter Crime?" *Social Science Quarterly*. 2015. Pdf. 28 Dec 2016.

Frostenson, Sarah. "Most Terrorist Attacks in the US Are Committed by Americans – Not Foreigners." *Vox*. Vox Media. Sep 9 2016. Web. 28 Dec 2016.

Gold, Liza H. *Gun Violence and Mental Illness*. New York: American Psychiatric Publishing, Inc, 2015.

Grambsch, Patricia. "Regression to the Mean, Murder Rates, and Shall-Issue Laws." The American Statistician, Vol. 62, No. 4, 2008, 289–95.

"Growing Public Support for Gun Rights." *Pew Research*. Pew Research Center US Politics and Policy. Dec 10 2014. Web. 25 Dec 2016.

Halbrook, Stephen P. *The Founders' Second Amendment: Origins of the Right to Bear Arms*. Chicago: Ivan R. Dee, 2008.

Harcourt, Bernard E. "On Gun Registration, the NRA, Adolf Hitler, and Nazi Gun Laws: Exploding the Gun Culture Wars (A Call to Historians)." Fordham Law Review, Vol. 73, No. 2, Art. 11, 2004, 653–80.

Hill, Steven and Robert Richie. "Why America Can't Pass Gun Control." *The Atlantic*. Atlantic Monthly Group. Dec 20 2012. Web. 28 Dec 2016.

Hiltzik, Michael. "The NRA Has Blocked Gun Violence Research for 20 Years. Let's End Its Stranglehold on Science." *Los Angeles Times*. Times Media. Jun 14 2016. Web. 1 Jan 2017.

"Identify Prohibited Persons." *ATF*. Bureau of Alcohol Tobacco and Firearms. Sep 22 2016. Web. 27 Dec 2016.

Ingraham, Christopher. "Guns Are Now Killing as Many People as Cars in the U.S." *Washington Post*. Nash Holdings. Dec 17 2015. Web. 28 Dec 2016.

———. "There Are Now More Guns Than People in the United States." *The Washington Post*. Oct 5 2015. Web. 27 Dec 2016.

Karp, Aaron. "Small Arms Survey 2007." *Small Arms Survey*. 2007. Pdf. 27 Dec 2016.

Kelto, Anders. "The US is a World Leader in Gun Deaths." *NPR*. National Public Radio. Dec 7 2015. Web. 27 Dec 2016.

Krause, William J. "Gun Control Legislation." *Congressional Research Service*. Federation of American Scientists. Nov 14 2016. Web. 28 Dec 2016.

Lane, Melissa. "How the Greeks Viewed Weapons." *The New Yorker*. Condé Nast. Feb 1 2013. Web. 25 Dec 2016.

Lott, John R. "Guns and the New York Times: Why Shouldn't Americans Be Able to Defend Themselves?" *Fox News*. Fox News Inc. Feb 24 2015. Web. 26 Dec 2016.

Masters, Jonathan. "Gun Control around the World: A Primer." *The Atlantic*. Atlantic Monthly Group. Jan 12 2016. Web. 28 Dec 2016.

Masters, Kate. "Just How Many People Get Guns without a Background Check? Fast-Tracked Research Is Set to Provide an Answer." *The Trace*. Oct 21 2015. Web. 27 Dec 2016.

———. "The CDC Just Released a 'Gun Violence' Study." *The Trace*. Dec 2 2015. Web. 28 Dec 2016.

McDonough, Katie. "Here's What US Gun Laws Would Look Like if a Majority of Americans Had Their Say." *Fusion*. Fusion Media Network, LLC. Aug 27 2015. Web. 29 Dec 2016.

Metzl, Jonathan and Kenneth T. MacLeish. "Mental Illness, Mass Shootings, and the Politics of American Firearms." American Journal of Public Health, Vol. 105, No. 2, 2015, 240-49.

Mika, Shelley. "Britons Aim for Tougher Gun Laws." *Gallup*. Gallup Inc. Jun 21 2005. Web. 28 Dec 2016.

Morin, Rich. "The Demographics and Politics of Gun Owning Households." *Pew Research Center*. Pew Foundation. Jul 15 2014. Web. 28 Dec 2016.

O'Brien, Kerry, Forrest, Walter, Lynott, Dermot, and Michael Daly. "Racism, Gun Ownership and Gun Control: Biased Attitudes in US Whites May Influence Policy Decisions." *PLOS*. PLOS. Oct 31 2013. Web. 28 Dec 2016.

"Opinions on Gun Policy and the 2016 Campaign." *Pew Research*. Pew Research Center US Politics & Policy. Aug 26, 2016. Web. 25 Dec 2016.

Parker, Clifton B. "Right-to-carry gun laws linked to increase in violent crime, Stanford research shows." *Stanford News*. Stanford University. Nov 14, 2014. Web.

Patel, Faiza and Adrienne Tierney. "The Reasons Why Dylann Roof Wasn't Charged with Terrorism." *Just Security*. New York University School of Law. Jul 30 2015. Web. 28 Dec 2016.

Raymond, Emilie. *From My Cold, Dead Hands: Charlton Heston and American Politics*. Lexington, University Press of Kentucky, 2006.

Ruben, Eric M. and Saul Cornell. "Firearm Regionalism and Public Carry: Placing Southern Antebellum Case Law in Context." *The Yale Law Journal*. Vol. 125. Sep 25, 2015. Web. 25 Dec 2016.

Slattery, Denis. "Most Americans Want Stricter Gun Control, But Doubt It'll Happen." *New York Daily News*. Jul 23 2016. Web. 28 Dec 2016.

Smith, Candace, Kelsey, Adam, and Veronica Stracqualursi. "Trump Says Maybe

'2nd Amendment People' Can Stop Clinton's Supreme Court Picks." *ABC News*. ABC. Aug 9 2016. Web. 28 Dec 2016.

Swanson, Jeffery W., et al. "Guns, Impulsive Angry Behavior, and Mental Disorders: Results from the National Comorbidity Survey Replication (NCS-R)." Behavioral Sciences & the Law, Vol. 33, Nos. 2-3, June, 2015, 199-212.

Swift, Art. "In U.S., Support for Assault Weapons Ban at Record Low." *Gallup*. Gallup, Inc. Oct 26 2016. Web. 27 Dec 2016.

"Ten Reasons Why States Should Reject 'Assault Weapon' and 'Large' Magazine Bans." *NRA-ILA*. Jun 17 2014. Web. 26 Dec 2016.

Valenti, Jessica. "Why Don't Americans Call Mass Shootings 'Terrorism'? Racism." *The Guardian*. Guardian News and Media. Jun 19 2015. Web. 29 Dec 2016.

"*United States v. Miller* 307 US 174 (1939)." *Supreme Justia*. Justia. 2016. Web. 27 Dec 2016.

Vizzard, William J. "The Current and Future State of Gun Policy in the United States." Journal of Criminal Law and Criminology, Vol. 104, No. 4, Art. 5, Fall, 2015, 879-904.

Weeks, Linton. "The First Gun in America." *NPR*. National Public Radio. Apr 6 2013. Web. 25 Dec 2016.

Weinstein, Adam. "The NRA Was Waging War on Facts Long Before the 'Fake News' Boom." *The Trace*. Dec 12 2016. Web. 29 Dec 2016.

Wellford, Charles F., Pepper, John V. and Carol V. Petrie. *Firearms and Violence: A Critical Review*. Washington D.C.: The National Academies Press, 2004.

"Why Are Americans Buying So Many Guns?" *Rasmussen Reports*. Rasmussen Reports, LLC. Apr 13 2016. Web. 26 Dec 2016.

"Why Own a Gun? Protection Is Now Top Reason." *Pew Research Center*. Pew Foundation. Mar 12 2013. Web. 28 Dec 2016.

Wilkinson, Peter. "Dunblane: How UK School Massacre Led to Tighter Gun Control." *CNN*. Cable News Network. Jan 30 2013. Web. 28 Dec 2016.

Wilson, Jason. "Extremist Militias Recruiting in Fear of Clinton Winning Election, Activists Say." *The Guardian*. Guardian News and Media. Oct 18 2016. Web. 28 Dec 2016.

Ye Hee Lee, Michelle. "Giuliani's Claim that 93 Percent of Black Murder Victims are Killed by Other Blacks." *The Washington Post*. Nash Holdings. No 25 2014. Web. 28 Dec 2016.

Zafirovsky, Milan and Daniel G. Rodeheaver. *Modernity and Terrorism*. Boston: Brill Publishers, 2013.

Zucchino, David. "A Militia Gets Battle Ready for a 'Gun-Grabbing' Clinton Presidency." *New York Times*. New York Times Co. Nov 4 2016. Web. 25 Dec 2016.

Websites

National Rifle Association
www.nra.org

The National Rifle Association (NRA) is a gun-rights advocacy group and gun industry lobbyist organization active since 1871, making it one of the nation's oldest rights-activist organizations. The NRA is currently considered one of the nation's most powerful lobbyist groups and publishes studies and articles on a variety of subjects. The NRA is supported by commercial entities involved in the sale of firearms, ammunition, and related equipment and so does not disseminate any information that might negatively impact the firearms industry and often actively endeavors to discourage confidence in information that negatively reflects on firearms ownership or usage.

National Association for Gun Rights
www.nationalgunrights.org

The NAGR is an activist organization that seeks to eliminate gun-control laws and publishes articles on the benefits of civilian gun ownership. All information provided and supported by the organization is extremely biased against gun control and the organization's website contains numerous alarmist claims about individuals and organizations that allegedly want to completely eliminate Second Amendment freedoms in the United States. While an interesting source of information, the NAGR is a lobbyist organization and not a research organization and information provided should not be considered a legitimate unless corroborated by independent sources.

Constitutional Rights Pac
www.constitutionalrightspac.com

The Constitutional Rights PAC, formerly known as the Revolution SuperPAC, is a political action committee that collects and donates funds to political candidates towards a variety of goals. The organization has been active in promoting extremist propaganda about gun-rights, including illegitimate claims connecting gun-control laws to historical dictatorships and authoritarian powers. Information promoted and presented by the organization should be considered highly suspect and no publication or article presented by the organization should be considered legitimate unless corroborated by independent sources.

Centers for Disease Control and Prevention
www.CDC.gov

Federal agency under the Department of Health and Human Services charged with studying and creating policy recommendations towards the goal of protecting public health. Though often targeted by gun-rights organizations as a biased institution in league with forces attempting to erode Second Amendment freedoms, the CDC is a nonpartisan government branch that works to combat disease around the world and has funded numerous, reputable studies on gun violence, injuries, and suicide.

The Trace
www.thetrace.org

The Trace is a journalistic organization founded in 2015 with funding from former New York City mayor Michael Bloomberg. The organization funds and publishes articles about the gun policy debate and provides information to publications writing articles about gun violence and gun-policy. Though distinctly in league with gun-control organizations, the Trace provides extensive links embedded in the articles published on the site, intended to allow readers to investigate the data and sources behind arguments made in the site's articles. While most of the articles published through the Trace support gun-control, the website also publishes articles in support of various gun rights perspectives and, particularly, in support of a moderate stance between gun rights and gun control.

Everytown for Gun Safety
www.everytown.org

Everytown for Gun Safety is a nonprofit organization advocating for gun control and for studies on the causes and effects of gun violence. The organization is co-chaired by former New York City mayor Michael Bloomberg and specifically promotes a moderate gun-control agenda that includes a campaign for universal background checks. The organization is nonpartisan, but strongly favors gun-control legislation.

Crime Prevention Research Center
www.crimeresearch.org

The Crime Prevention Research Center is a gun rights and anti-gun control activist organization started by conservative academic John Lott in the late 1990s. Articles and studies published by the organization attempt to delegitimize studies indicating that gun ownership does not enhance public safety. Though there are legitimate academic studies published by the organization, most information available through the website should be considered biased against most types of gun control.

Politifact

www.politifact.com

Organization that attempts to fact-check statements made by politicians and other public figures. The organization has been criticized as having both a liberal and conservative bias, by critics on either side of the debate, but evidence of bias has not been convincing. Politifact is helpful for researchers as the articles published by the website provide links to research cited in statements made by public figures and can therefore allow readers to conduct their own fact checking of controversial statements or persons.

Snopes

www.Snopes.com

Snopes is a website that publishes articles about rumors, online viral posts, and statements made by or about politicians and other public figures. Snopes has been accused of liberal bias and conservative bias, from those on both sides of the political divide, but makes the sources of its fact-checking activities available in each article and so provides an invaluable source of information for readers wishing to investigate the validity of various statements and Internet rumors. Due to the saturation of incorrect information in the firearms debate, readers are encouraged to use Snopes and similar websites to check arguments made by politicians and activists on both sides of the debate.

FactCheck.org

www.factcheck.org

FactCheck.org is a project of the Annenberg Public Policy Center that attempts to reduce misleading information and false claims in the US political system. Fact-Check.org has won numerous awards for journalistic integrity and provides a powerful resource for individuals looking to investigate the legitimacy of political claims. Articles published in FactCheck.org provide source information to allow users to independently verify the veracity of political statements against data used to make arguments. Due to the promulgation of false and misleading data in the gun-policy debate, users are encouraged to check statements and statistics given by politicians using FactCheck.org or similar websites.

Pew Research Center

www.pewresearch.org

One of the world's leading sources for popular polling data and studies on a wide variety of social and political topics. Pew Research Center is nonpartisan and regularly publishes articles and studies that could be described as supportive and/or critical of both conservative and liberal policies and behavior. The Pew Research Center is also one of the prime sources for data on public opinion, covering a variety of issues from the gun-policy debate to bias in popular media.

Index